3M

3M

CHINESE
AMERICANS

CHINESE AMERICANS:
THE IMMIGRANT EXPERIENCE

Dušanka Mišćević and
Peter Kwong

HUGH LAUTER LEVIN ASSOCIATES, INC.

Copyright © 2000
Hugh Lauter Levin Associates, Inc.
Series editor: Leslie C. Carola
Design: Ken Scaglia
Photo editor: Leslie C. Carola
Production editor: Deborah T. Zindell
Printed in Hong Kong
ISBN 0-88363-128-8
HTTP://WWW.HLLA.COM
DISTRIBUTED BY PUBLISHERS GROUP WEST

CONTENTS

CHINESE AMERICANS

I come from the East–China.
I am making a living in the West–America
With the Eastern mind:
Peace, freedom, harmony, tranquillity
Joy humility . . .
I paint.

Heaven, earth
Creativity grow.
Time, life
Inspiration flow.
Look, feel
I reflect
Subjectively, objectively
Form, formless;
I myself, no-self . . .
I paint.

"It is by the Odes that the mind is aroused.
It is by propriety that the character is established.
It is from music that perfection is attained."

Un-building
Re-building
Ever-building . . .
On and on
in Man's Garden
I paint.

CHEN CHI

Chen Chi. *July 4th Fireworks in New York*. 1982. Watercolor on paper. 35 x 38 in.

INTRODUCTION

The end of the twentieth century finds the Chinese thriving in America, experiencing what one has come to expect of a typical American immigrant success story. We find them in all walks of life, competing for elected political office, running universities and companies, winning Nobel Prizes in the sciences and Olympic medals in sports, performing on the nation's most prestigious music and theater stages, creating award-winning art and fashion, designing the latest computer hard- and software, and performing more ordinary jobs as engineers, lawyers, doctors, accountants, nurses, clerks, waiters, dishwashers, factory workers, and salespeople. In fact, so successful have they been in embodying the American dream that the Chinese Americans have been pronounced "a model minority"—as if to prove that America is a society where anybody can succeed, regardless of background or color. *Chinese Americans: The Immigrant Experience* celebrates the Chinese-American life, while also acknowledging the fact that the Chinese have had one of the most unique and painful experiences of the immigrant groups that have made America their home.

The Chinese were among the earliest immigrant groups to arrive in America—around the same time as the "Old Immigrants" (i.e. the Germans and the Irish), and much earlier than any of the southern and eastern Europeans. If America were the land of equal promise for all those who

(Opposite) **A Chinatown mural depicting the journey of Chinese immigrants to the United States, New York, 1996. Photo © 1996 Chien-Chi Chang/ Magnum Photos.**

The photographer captures an overworked immigrant in a rare moment of relaxation on a grimy Chinatown rooftop, while the dazzling Manhattan skyline in the background serves as a reminder of the "stuff the immigrant dreams are made of." Nothing could better embody the contrast between immigrant dreams and reality. Photo © 1998 Chien-Chi Chang/ Magnum Photos.

dared claim its opportunities, the Chinese should have experienced a path of assimilation and upward mobility similar to that of other immigrant groups—and they should have achieved it as early as the Germans and the Irish. Instead, they found themselves ostracized by means of exclusion and miscegenation laws and isolated in urban ghettos as undesirable aliens who were not given a chance to succeed, nor were they expected to assimilate. The history of the Chinese in America is a broken history—broken in 1882 by the Chinese Exclusion Act, and continued only after the act was repealed in 1943, when the Chinese were given the same access to immigration into the United States as any other nation of the world, and therefore, finally, the same chance to embark on a "typical American immigrant" path to success like their European counterparts.

There is no doubt that racial discrimination played an important part in the Chinese-American experience. But there is also no doubt that the Chinese have made the best of the opportunities they were given, whether poor peasants lured into indentured servitude by greedy employers, or the educated elite who took refuge in the United States during civil strife in

China. The extraordinary success of this last group has also tended to obscure the diversity within the Chinese-American community. While some Chinese Americans take pride in being singled out as the model minority, others continue to struggle in conditions unknown to most Americans, while still others yet insist that they feel a part of the American mainstream. This diversity among Chinese Americans is often ignored when only one aspect of their collective experience is emphasized, but in that sense they are no different from any other immigrant group within which one finds an entire social spectrum.

Chinese Americans: The Immigrant Experience presents the story of Chinese in America in all its multi-dimensional and colorful complexity: the community's scope and diversity, its suffering and struggles, and its hard-won triumphs and current achievements. The Chinese experience can teach a painful but important lesson about what it means to be American and what it takes to make it in America.

A Chinese immigrant is sworn in as a U.S. citizen in New York City, 1996. The provisions of the 1965 Immigration Act have brought an unprecedented number of highly skilled Chinese professionals to the United States, while allotting 74 percent of the immigration quota to the relatives of earlier immigrants of humble, rural origins. This has created an unnatural duality in the Chinese-American population. Photo © 1996 Chien-Chi Chang/ Magnum Photos.

EARLY SINO-AMERICAN CONTACTS

American interest in China antedates Chinese immigration to the Americas by more than a half century. Early Sino-American contacts are usually associated with profitable commerce. Indeed, one of the most compelling economic reasons for the American Revolution itself was the desire of American merchants and traders to wrest control of the China trade from the British. The tea dumped into Boston Harbor on December 16, 1773, by a group of Boston citizens to protest the British tax on tea imported to the colonies was, of course, Chinese tea. After independence from Great Britain, American ships began to engage in the lucrative tea trade. The celebrated voyage of the merchant ship *Empress of China* from New York to Canton in 1784, the first of its kind, returned a 30 percent profit on an investment of $120,000. Other ships soon followed: by 1790, the business community of every coastal city in the newly independent United States of America, from Salem, Massachusetts, to Norfolk, Virginia, sent at least one ship to Canton.

In addition to tea, wealthy Americans sought Chinese porcelain and art objects to decorate their homes following the tastes and fashions that had swept western Europe since the seventeenth century and which gave rise to a style in Western art commonly known as "Chinoiserie." Chinese luxury goods became particularly popular when Andreas Everard Van

(Previous spread) A contemporary Chinese farmer working in a field in Guangdong Province. Early Chinese immigrants came to America almost exclusively from a 4,000-square-mile area in Southern China, centered around the city of Guangzhou (Canton) in Guangdong Province.

(Opposite) A Chinese export porcelain plate with an image of the ship *Friendship* of Salem, Massachusetts, built in 1815 in Portland, Maine. Peabody Essex Museum, Salem, MA. Americans went to the trading port of Canton primarily to buy Chinese products prized in the United States and Europe.

Factories at Canton (from the Harbor), China. Unknown Chinese artist. c. 1850. Oil on canvas. 6 ⅞ x 10 ¾ in. Collection of The New-York Historical Society. The foreign trading enclosure at Canton with the Customs House. The American Factory is marked by the flag furthest to the left; the British East India Company is second from the right. Canton (today's Guangzhou, the capital of Guangdong Province) is a southern Chinese port city in the Pearl River Delta near the South China Sea, where the British established the first "factory," or trading post, in 1699, for the purpose of conducting the lucrative China tea trade. Other Western traders soon followed. The Qing government restricted its foreign trade with Western nations to the city of Canton, where the foreign merchants were obliged to live and conduct business in a riverbank area outside the city walls, known as the "Thirteen Factories."

Braam Houckgeest, after a successful mercantile-diplomatic sojourn in China, settled in America in 1796 and built his "China Retreat" on the Delaware River just above Philadelphia. The estate included a Chinese pagoda where he exhibited his vast collection of Chinese paintings and art objects—undoubtedly the first comprehensive Chinese collection seen in America. (The collection was auctioned off by Christie's in 1799.) Van Braam also brought with him voluminous notes for the first work on China to be published in America (in French, in the years 1798 and 1799), and a monogrammed Chinese porcelain tea service for the First Lady of the United States, Martha Washington. Soon, every respectable home of means in the eastern United States aspired to acquire its own set of Chinese porcelain and its own collection of Chinese silks, rugs, and art objects.

Chinese porcelain cake plate. c. 1795. Diameter: 13 7/8 in. Courtesy, Winterthur Museum. Presented in 1796 to Martha Washington by A. E. Van Braam Houckgeest upon his return from China.

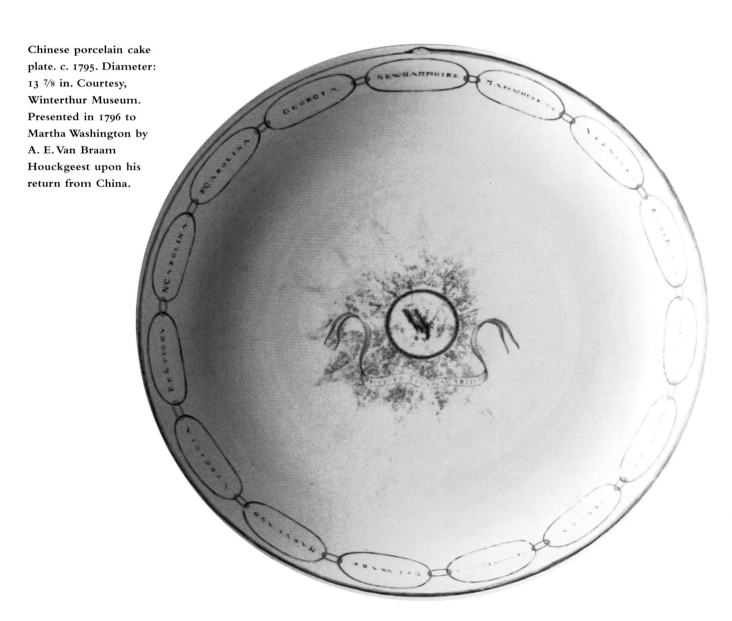

The importance of the China trade to the new republic is best demonstrated by the fact that one of the very first consulates it established after independence was the one in Canton, in southern China. Major Samuel Shaw was appointed as the United States Consul at Canton as early as 1786.

Based on these early, limited contacts, eighteenth-century Americans developed perceptions of China markedly different from the attitudes that took shape later, in the nineteenth and early twentieth centuries. The Philadelphia intelligensia, influenced by the views of the philosophers of the European Enlightenment, approached China as a source of inspiration and innovation. Benjamin Franklin looked to China for new ideas and methods on topics as varied as census-taking, silk production, windmills, and heating systems. James Madison admired Chinese intensive agricultural techniques. Thomas Jefferson envied China's political and commercial isolation—a position he wished the United States could assume relative to Europe. James Monroe drew inspiration for his famous doctrine from his view of China as a nation "perfectly independent" of the world powers.

The American Ship **Challenge** *With Hong Kong in the Background.* **Hong Kong artist Hin Qua. Late 19th century. Oil on canvas. Peabody Essex Museum, Salem, MA.**

Further contacts with China in the nineteenth century slowly changed such admiring, respectful views. China's economic and military power steadily declined throughout the nineteenth century, while technological invention and industrial development proceeded apace in the United States. From the 1840s onward China was plunged into domestic and foreign crisis, and Americans began to view it as a backward, stagnant country of weak, inept, and despotic rulers. One of the chief evils afflicting Chinese society was opium.

(Right) **Chinese export-porcelain soup plate. c. 1830–40. Peabody Essex Museum, Salem, MA. Porcelains from the imperial kilns at Jingdezhen in Jiangxi Province were prized by Chinese connoisseurs long before they became a European, and then American, vogue. They reached their height of perfection with Ming blue-and-white and Qing polychrome wares. During the 18th and 19th centuries lower quality porcelains were mass produced for export to the West.**

(Following spread) Whampoa (Huangpu) Reach, China. **Unknown Chinese artist. c. 1850. Peabody Essex Museum, Salem, MA. The Treaty of Nanjing (1842) opened five of China's ports— Canton, Fuzhou, Xiamen, Ningbo, and Shanghai—to foreign trade. Shanghai, located on the lower reaches of the Huangpu River, was particularly attractive to foreign traders because it was close to the areas of tea and silk production. The painting was probably commissioned by an American living there.**

Qing Dynasty Robe. 18th century. Blue silk warp twill with ornament in couched, wrapped gold and silver yarns; pale blue eyes for dragons. Length: 56 ⅝ in. The Metropolitan Museum of Art, Gift of Lewis Einstein, 1954. For many centuries silkworm cultivation and silk weaving were secret processes, known only to the Chinese. Already during the Roman Empire camel caravans traveled from China to the Middle East to sell the coveted cloth to the Western world. Although by the Qing dynasty the Chinese no longer enjoyed a monopoly on its production, they still made the best-quality silks in the world, much coveted by the foreign traders at Canton.

"Pride of China." Posters advertising Chinese tea by the D. H. Houghtaling & Co., importers of fine teas from the Orient.
By the end of the eighteenth century, tea had become America's most popular drink. Tea was the main reason American merchants
went to China. The American Revolution itself was fought over the British taxation of Chinese tea. Shipment of the precious,
perishable tea leaves to the East Coast became much more cost-effective with the opening of the Suez Canal in 1869.

CHINA TRADE AND
THE OPIUM WARS

Early trade between China and the United States was lopsided. Americans went to the trading port of Canton primarily to buy Chinese products prized in the United States and Europe: silks, nankeen cotton cloth, porcelain, and above all tea. (Tea had become part of the daily fare in New England as early as the 1720s, and by the early 1780s most Americans had acquired the tea-drinking habit.) There was very little that the Chinese wanted in exchange. New England ginseng was of inferior grade. Sea-otter skins, seal pelts, and sandalwood obtained from Hawaii were never plentiful enough, and their sources were soon depleted. The balance in trade was made up in specie—the Spanish silver dollars and bullion, usually difficult to assemble in sufficient quantity—until Americans discovered the ideal medium of exchange: opium.

Opium was first introduced into the China trade by the British East India Company, desperate to improve its trade balance sheets. (The silver flow into China grew from 3 million teals in the 1760s, to 7.5 million teals in the 1770s, to 16 million teals in the 1780s.) Opium was grown in British-ruled India and illegally brought by select licensed Western merchants for trading to Canton. American merchants were mostly excluded from trading in Indian opium, but they soon located an alternative source in the Turkish port of Smyrna. Philadelphia and Baltimore ships traded in Turkish

(Opposite) The Bombardment of Canton by the English Under Captain Elliott. 1841. Woodcut. **The First Anglo-Chinese War of 1839–42, better known as the Opium War, has provided more occasion for the charge of "imperialist aggression" than any other episode in modern history. It was precipitated by the Chinese government's effort to suppress the illicit trade in opium conducted by British merchants in the port city of Guangzhou (Canton). British warships attacked Canton to prove the superior power of Western innovative military technology and tactics.**

SHANG H

(Previous spread) Shanghai, China. **Unknown Chinese artist. Oil on canvas. Peabody Essex Museum, Salem, MA. Shanghai was merely a small fishing village when it was first opened to foreign trade in 1843. It soon grew into a major international trading center— a distinction it holds to this very day. Foreign trading companies crowded its waterfront. Here, the United States flag flies third from right.**

(Opposite) **Poster advertisement for the shipping services provided by the Glidden & Williams' line aboard its "splendid new A.I. Clipper Bark *Pekin*." American trading companies vied with other Western merchants for the lucrative China trade.**

opium as early as 1804. By 1817-1818, Turkish opium accounted for half the goods brought by Americans into Canton. By the 1820s, Americans were carrying as much as 2,000 chests (133 tons) of opium annually. Some of the most prominent American trading firms of the day made their fortunes in opium, including Wetmore and Oliphant, Browns of Providence, Astor of New York, and Girard of Philadelphia. And while the above-mentioned got out of handling opium in 1836, Perkins and Company and its successor, Russell and Company, went on to accumulate small fortunes for their agents, whose names still resonate with success even today: Perkins, Heard, Low, Hunter, Forbes, Delano, Sturgis, and King. Most writers of American history tend to conveniently overlook the fact that some of the most prominent "blue-blooded" families of the formative age of American capitalism accumulated their wealth in the opium trade, which today would be considered exploitive if not immoral and certainly illegal.

In the nineteenth century, the opium trade was in fact illegal—in China, that is. The imperial Qing government banned it as soon as its destructive effects on Chinese society became evident and repeatedly lodged protests with Western governments over the continuing unauthorized activities of Western traders on moral grounds. In 1838, Chinese emperor Daoguang appointed a scholar-official named Lin Zexu as an imperial commissioner to Canton—to which the Western traders were restricted by imperial foreign trade regulations—with the task of ending the practice. Commissioner Lin issued proclamations, made hundreds of arrests, and confiscated thousands of pounds of opium and opium pipes from his Chinese subjects. When his pleas to foreign opium traders—the majority of them being British and American—to hand over their merchandise went unanswered, he blockaded the 350 foreigners in Canton in their warehouses for six weeks, until they gave up over 20,000 chests. As a large crowd of Chinese and foreigners watched, the 3 million pounds of raw opium contained in those chests were dissolved in water, salt, and lime, and washed out to sea. To conclude the episode, Commissioner Lin wrote a memorial to the emperor in which he suggested that the foreigners "do not dare show any disrespect, and indeed I should judge from their attitudes that they have the decency to feel heartily ashamed."

GLIDDEN & WILLIAMS' LINE
FOR SAN FRANCISCO
FROM LEWIS WHARF.
THE SPLENDID NEW A1 CLIPPER BARK

W. F. SEYMOUR, Commander.

This vessel is now in berth with a portion of her cargo on board. She is very sharp, of beautiful model, and as she will carry but a small cargo, shippers will much oblige by the prompt delivery of their engagements, especially heavy goods.

For Freight, apply at the California Packet Office, No. 114 State Street, Boston.

British warships attack and overwhelm the obsolete Chinese junks and guns at Chapu near the mouth of the Yangtze River above Shanghai in another incident of the Opium War, on May 18, 1841.

He couldn't have been more wrong. The British response was swift. The full British fleet arrived off Canton, and proceeded north up the Chinese coast blockading all major ports. By 1842, several ports had been captured and all main river and canal communications in China's interior cut. The Manchu government capitulated, opening five Chinese ports—Canton, Fuzhou, Xiamen, Ningbo, and Shanghai—to residence by British subjects "for the purpose of carrying on their mercantile pursuits, without molestation or restraint . . . with whatever persons they please," and ceding possession of the Island of Hong Kong to Queen Victoria and her descendents "in perpetuity." The Opium Wars of 1839-42 and the resulting Treaty of Nanjing (1842) marked an important historical moment. They confirmed the superior power of Western innovative military technology and tactics and forced China to sign similarly unequal treaties with a number of Western trading nations. American congressman Caleb Cushing of Massachusetts was dispatched by President John Tyler in 1843 to work out a favorable trading arrangement for wealthy American China merchants, the majority of whom lived in Massachusetts. The Treaty of Wangxia, which gave United States citizens in China the same rights enjoyed by British subjects in the five treaty ports, was signed in 1844. But the American treaty also included a few significant additions. The Americans had the right to construct hospitals, churches, and cemeteries, to employ people from any part of China, and to be tried and punished only by duly empowered American officials

"according to the laws of the United States"—in other words, in a jurisdictional sense, United States citizens in China were to enjoy extra-territorial rights.

The opening of Chinese ports to unrestricted foreign trade resulted in the
free flow of opium into China—although the trading of opium was still
technically illegal—which soon tipped the balance of trade in favor of the
aggressive Western nations. The opium trade weakened the country economically and, by the end of the nineteenth century, brought the ruling
Manchu Qing dynasty to the verge of social disintegration and complete
political collapse.

Boats from British navy warships *Sulphur, Calliope, Larne,* and *Starling* help the British East India Company's iron-hulled, paddle-wheel steamer, *Nemesis,* attack and destroy a Chinese fleet of junks in shallow water of the Canton Bogue near Chuenpi (Anson's Bay) on January 7, 1841.

British soldiers called "Victorian Vikings" attack and capture the Chuenpi fort—one of several fortifications protecting the city of Canton, as British warships destroy the Chinese fleet in the shallow waters near Chuenpi on January 7, 1841. The defeat forced local Chinese officials to agree to cede Hong Kong, pay war indemnities, and open official contact between Britain and the Qing government.

Engraving of the British seizure of Canton in December 1857, during a bombardment campaign. The Treaty of Nanjing was signed on August 29, 1842, ending the First Opium War. Hostilities continued, however, as each Western power demanded the most-favored-nation status granted Americans in 1844, which allowed United States citizens to reside in China's open ports "according to the laws of the United States"— namely, in jurisdictional sense, extra-territorial rights.

CAUSES OF CHINESE MIGRATION: THE PUSH-PULL THEORY

The economic and social decline that imperial China experienced during the second half of the nineteenth century created the "push factor" in Chinese emigration to America and other parts of the world. The Qing government, which had previously strictly controlled the movement of its subjects, could no longer prevent an exodus of Chinese people, now that five of China's chief port cities were under the control of foreign powers. Many coastal Chinese, exposed to the outside world due to their contacts with foreign nationals who resided in the five ports, wanted to leave China for better economic opportunities overseas.

In addition, China was plagued by domestic rebellion. The most famous of the uprisings was the Christian-influenced Taiping Rebellion (1850–1864), which was dedicated to religious reform and overthrow of the Manchus. It caused the death of some 20 million people and laid waste huge areas of what had once been China's most prosperous region. Another uprising, the

Red Turban Rebellion, directly affected eight coastal counties around the city of Canton, from which came the majority of early Chinese immigrants to the United States. Clearly, the rebellions provided an additional "push" to emigration.

The "pull" was provided by the Western colonial powers in need of an ever larger number of cheap and subservient laborers to develop their newly acquired territories in the New World. In fact, due to the worldwide effort to abolish slavery, United States employers were so concerned with the supply of labor from China that Anson Burlingame, who had served as ambassador to China from 1861 to 1867, persuaded the United States government to sign the Burlingame Treaty with China in 1868, to ensure that nationals from either country could emigrate and immigrate without restrictions.

Most of the early Chinese immigrants to the U.S. came almost exclusively from a four-thousand-square-mile area in southern China, centered around the city of Canton. This was the area first opened to foreign trade, and its local residents benefited from their foreign contacts by becoming merchants and assistants to foreign traders, as well as their household servants, interpreters, Christian missionaries' Bible peddlers, and sailors on foreign ships. They later facilitated labor recruitment for the New World by becoming contractors for their colonial masters. Recruitment was relatively easy. Able-bodied men were recruited under a "credit ticket" system, which gave them deferred-payment sea passage to America. In exchange, they were often forced to work in conditions of indentured servitude after their arrival in the United States to pay back their transportation debts. They came to be known as "coolies" in English, after a Hindi word for a hired servant, since they were recruited to perform strenuous menial work for little pay. But in their own minds they must have thought that the appellation was plucked from their own language, because "ku-li" means "bitter strength" in Chinese, and nothing seemed to fit their experience more perfectly than that term.

Reception of the Hon. Anson Burlingame and members of the Chinese Embassy, by the Traveler's Club, May 30, 1868. **Burlingame, who had served as the United States minister to China from 1861 to 1867, was assigned by the Qing court in 1868 to represent China in treaty discussions in the United States and Europe.**

Between 1850 and 1900 some half a million Chinese journeyed to the United States in search of work. This number was not small: in California, a quarter of the male able-bodied labor force was Chinese by 1870. But

Chinese migration to the United States was only a small part—no more than one-tenth—of the greater Chinese exodus that was gaining momentum after the Opium Wars. In response to the opportunities created by Western trade and capital expansion and by the new technologies employed in the mines, railways, and plantations of the colonies of Southeast Asia, Australia, and the Americas, many more emigrants left southern coastal China for the Malay peninsula, Indochina, Sumatra, Java, the Philippines, Hawaii, the West Indies, Peru, Cuba, Mexico, and Panama. It has been estimated that during the period from 1847 to 1874, between a quarter- to a half-million Chinese laborers were shipped from the port cities of Xiamen, Canton, and Hong Kong to plantations in Cuba, Peru, Chile, and the Sandwich Islands alone.

During the visit of a group of senior Qing officials to the United States in 1868, Anson Burlingame persuaded the U.S. government to sign a treaty with China (known as The Burlingame Treaty), which ensured that nationals from either country could emigrate and immigrate without restrictions.

EARLY CHINESE IMMIGRATION

The earliest written record of the presence of Chinese in North America involves a case of stranded Asian seamen who landed in Baltimore in August 1785 aboard the ship named *Pallas*. The three "natives of China" among the crew spent over a year in Philadelphia waiting to be hired by a ship bound for Asia. It is not known exactly when and how they left America.

The next record is of five Chinese servants accompanying Andreas Everard Van Braam Houckgeest, the merchant-diplomat and collector of Chinese art who settled in America in 1796. Again, it is not known what happened to the five men after Van Braam died in Amsterdam in 1801.

Chances are that there were other Chinese in East Coast ports at least as early as this, but their presence would not have been mentioned in the newly independent and rapidly expanding nation unless they played a significant role in the economic or political life of the time. There are, however, a number of accounts of Chinese in the post-Revolutionary life on the Pacific Coast. John Meares, a former lieutenant in the Royal Navy, left military service in 1786 to engage in commerce between Canton and the North American Pacific Coast. He sailed from Canton in 1788 with some fifty Chinese on board, and brought them to Nootka Sound (two hundred miles northwest of present-day Vancouver, Canada) to establish a

(Previous spread) The Port of Canton. Artist unknown. Late 19th century. Oil on canvas. Flags flying over the waterfront demonstrate the presence of several Western nations in the busy port of Canton.

(Opposite) Chinese immigrants arrive at the San Francisco Custom House in 1877. Between 1850 and 1900 some half a million Chinese journeyed to the United States in search of work. For practical reasons American employers in California brought Chinese workers to California from across the Pacific. Consequently, most of the early Chinese immigrants first set foot on American soil in the port city of San Francisco.

fur-trading base. The Chinese built a stockade and set to work as smiths and armorers, constructing the forty-ton *North West American*—the first sailing vessel of its kind known to have been built on the Pacific Coast. In 1789, at least two other ships left Canton with Chinese on board: *Eleanor* with forty-five and *Argonaut* with twenty-nine, the latter bearing seven carpenters, five blacksmiths, five bricklayers-masons, four tailors, four shoemakers, three seamen, and one cook—all destined for the fur-trading settlement of Nootka.

Since there were no newspapers and few chroniclers of events on the West Coast aside from ships' captains, most accounts of the early Chinese presence in America come largely from East Coast sources. Thus we know that there was a near-continuous but not large presence of Chinese on the East Coast from around 1800 to 1848. In 1800, a veteran commander of several ships in the China trade, James Magee, brought a Chinese student to Rhode Island to see a part of the United States, learn the language, and eventually return to China in two to three years. A circus performing at the corner of Broadway and Anthony streets in 1808 featured a young Chinese "over his horse in full speed." In 1809, John Jacob Astor petitioned Thomas Jefferson on behalf of one of his Chinese crewmen needing return passage to his homeland. In 1813, a Chinese from the vessel *Sally* attended church services at Plymouth, Massachusetts, "in full Mandarin costume." In 1818, a church-run school for foreigners at Cornwall, Connecticut, took in five Chinese students. In 1830, the Bostonian John P. Cushing returned from thirty years' residence in Canton with a retinue of Chinese servants. A Chinese juggler called Ah Fong performed in New York in 1842. And then in 1845, Atit, a Cantonese who had resided in Boston for eight years, became a citizen of the United States.

Perhaps the most famous Chinese to take up residence in the United States during the period, however, were the three Chinese students who arrived in 1847 with the Reverend Samuel R. Brown, an educator with the Morrison Education Society in Macao and Hong Kong. All three had previously been Brown's students, and were scheduled for a two-year stay at the Monson Academy in Monson, Massachusetts, to study Western science

and technology. All three went on to play important roles in educating both Americans and Chinese about each other. The best known was Yung Wing, who came from a small village near Macao on the South China Coast. After Monson Academy he entered Yale University in 1850, was naturalized in New Haven in 1852, and in 1854 became the first Chinese to graduate from an American university. He spent the following five decades on often frustrated efforts to introduce Western science and technology to China and to expose Chinese youth to Western education. At his urging, the Qing government established an Overseas Bureau and appointed him to head the Chinese Educational Mission to the United States. In this capacity, starting in 1872, he brought 120 Chinese students to study science and technology at eastern colleges and universities. The program, which produced the first crop of Western-trained mining and railroad engineers in China, was considered destructive to Chinese culture and morals by conservatives in China, who forced the Qing government to stop it in 1881, when the American government refused to honor its treaty agreements to allow Chinese students to enter military academies at West Point and Annapolis. Yung Wing was stripped of his American citizenship in 1898, when he sought official support from the United States for a railway concession on behalf of the Chinese government—which was considered a violation of

"Marketing at the Five Points Section, New York City." Frank Leslie's Illustrated Newspaper, **May 1869. Five Points, the infamous slum located on the southern tip of Manhattan, housed wave upon wave of poor immigrants "mostly the Irish in the 1840's and 1850's" when they first settled in the city. In 1850, only 150 Chinese lived in lower Manhattan; in 1880 their quarter on Mott Street numbered no more than 700. Most made a living as sailors, cooks, domestic servants, and entertainers, but a few were also tea merchants and peddlers—like the Chinese man with the pushcart piled with fish and vegetables seen here, lower left.**

U.S. law. But he was married to a daughter of an American doctor, and he continued to travel between the two countries, never quite relinquishing his mission as a bridge between the two cultures. Both of his sons were educated at Yale. Mark Twain was a personal friend, which is one reason why Twain avoided and even spoofed the stereotyped views about Chinese that were being fostered in the America of his time.

In the middle of the nineteenth century the numbers of Chinese in the United States were very small. *The New York Times* estimated that in 1850, only 150 Chinese lived on the Lower East Side of Manhattan. In addition to the sailors, cooks, domestic servants, and entertainers already mentioned, the small community also included tea merchants and peddlers, as well as indentured laborers who had escaped from plantations in Cuba and Peru. This was the beginning of the first permanent Chinese settlement on the

Students from China brought to the U.S. to study, 1872. The first Chinese student to graduate from an American university (Yale, 1854), Yung Wing, seated second from right, founded the Chinese Educational Mission.

East Coast. In comparison, there were 4,018 Chinese men (and 7 Chinese women) in San Francisco that same year.

Then something dramatic happened. With the opening of the West and the incorporation of California, where gold was found, the need for cheap labor soared. This was the time of the raging national debates on the abolition of slavery that preceded the Civil War. The use of black slave labor was a sensitive issue, and employing black slave labor was out of the question in the newly incorporated state of California, since it had joined the Union as a free state (as states that banned slavery were known). In addition, without a transcontinental railroad, the movement of any kind of workers around Cape Horn from the Eastern seaboard would have been uneconomical, as it would have been to move them overland by wagon train. It seemed much more practical to bring Chinese workers from across the Pacific. They were cheap and well-disciplined, and could be obtained in unlimited numbers. By the mid-1850s Chinese were arriving in California by the thousands. In 1860, there were 33,149 Chinese men in San Francisco alone. By 1870, 25 percent of the able-bodied male population in California was Chinese.

In the Schoolroom. **The Chinese College at Hartford, Connecticut, c. 1878. The college was established to accommodate the 120 Chinese students brought by Yung Wing to study in America. They lived with local families who volunteered to serve as their hosts.**

(Opposite) **Chinese residents of San Francisco celebrate the Chinese Lunar New Year, c. 1880, in the traditional way—by setting off firecrackers. During the second half of the 19th century the Chinese population of San Francisco grew by leaps and bounds. In 1850, there were only 4,025 Chinese in the city; by 1860, their numbers had reached almost 35,000.**

(Left) **Chinese laborers at work on the Milloudon Sugar Plantation in Louisiana, 1871. In July 1869, a convention of Southern planters and business-men met in Memphis, Tennessee, to discuss the feasibility of encouraging the hard-working Chinese to come to the South. By 1870, at least two hundred Chinese work-ers were employed in the cotton fields of the Yazoo-Mississippi Delta region of Mississippi and Arkansas.**

Chinese laborers were initially recruited to work in the gold mines on the West Coast. Later, as the transcontinental railroads began to be built in the 1860s, they were also sought by the railroad companies. For instance, when the Central Pacific Railroad was chartered in California to build the west-ern section of the projected transcontinental rail link, its head of construc-tion, Charles Crocker, approached the Chinese Six Companies, which were recruiting Chinese workers at thirty-five dollars per head from California and China, to supply nine thousand of the estimated ten thousand laborers that the project would require.

The work ethic of the Chinese evidently caught the attention of employ-ers elsewhere in the country as well. By the late 1860s, when Southern plantation owners grew anxious to replace what they considered to be "complacent and emancipated" black slaves, they too tried to recruit the Chinese to work in agriculture. Chinese workers were likewise in demand in the North. In 1870, records show, Chinese were sought to work as strike breakers in Calvin T. Sampson's shoe factories in North Adams,

Massachusetts; to counter strikes by Irish workers in Passaic Steam Laundry in Belleville, New Jersey; and to help discipline striking white workers in the Beaver Falls Cutlery Company in Beaver Falls, Pennsylvania. A writer for *Scribner's Monthly* commented: "If for no other purpose than the breaking up of the incipient steps toward labor combinations and 'Trade Unions' . . . the advent of Chinese labor should be hailed with warm welcome." The Chinese, he concluded, could be the "final solution" to the labor problem in America.

But white workers were much less welcoming of the Asian intruders than their white employers. In North Adams, "A large and hostile crowd met them at the depot, hooted them, hustled them somewhat, and threw stones at them," according to *The Nation*. Before long, hiring Chinese workers became a "national issue."

Teaching the newly recruited Chinese workers how to use the pegging machine at the Calvin T. Sampson shoe factory in North Adams, Massachusetts, 1870. Considered cheap labor, many Chinese were brought to work as strike breakers in the factories.

IN SEARCH OF OPPORTUNITIES IN THE NEW WORLD
MINING

The reason so many laborers left southern coastal China for the United States during the second half of the nineteenth century was because they were promised work. Most of the first migrants were bound for California's gold mines, and the promise of the New World is embodied in the Chinese name for San Francisco—the first place where most early Chinese immigrants set foot on the American continent: "The Nine Hills of Gold." Undoubtedly, the name conjured images of streets paved with gold, and in that sense the Chinese were no different from any other ethnic group during the Gold Rush. The Gum Sann, as it is called in Cantonese, or "Gold Mountain" of California, had captured not only the imagination of the Chinese but of the whole world.

The daily experience of Chinese laborers in California's gold mines was far from a fairy tale, however. During the first few years of individual surface

A photograph of the employees in front of the Sampson shoe factory in North Adams, Massachusetts, in the 1870s, shows that many of them were Chinese.

53

Chinese immigrants in California panning for gold. The promise of work lured many laborers from southern coastal China to the United States during the second half of the 19th century. Most of the first migrants headed for California's gold mines. The promise of the New World is embodied in the Chinese name for San Francisco—the first place where most early Chinese immigrants set foot on the American continent—"The Nine Hills of Gold." Life in the mining camps was quite different, however. The Chinese were forced to rework the claims abandoned by white miners, and were often attacked by the marauding outlaws if they struck a good return.

Chinese and white miners working side by side at the head of Auburn Ravine in California, in 1852. In 1851, large-scale company mining began to replace small claims of individual surface diggers, who depended on natural waterways to pan for gold. Company owners quickly turned to China for cheap labor, and before the end of 1852, over 20,000 Chinese were brought to California to work in company mines.

mining in California, very few Chinese were there. Of the 57,787 miners in the state in 1850, only about 500 were Chinese. As relative newcomers to the area, they were forced to perform the most backbreaking work on poor, two-dollar-a-day claims, in harsh conditions and subject to attacks by marauding outlaws. (The largest congregation of Chinese miners in one district was twenty-three, according to the 1850 census, averaging about three persons in each dwelling.) If they happened to strike a rich lead, they were immediately driven off. The first incident of anti-Chinese rioting occurred in 1849, when a party of white miners attacked some sixty Chinese miners who were working for a British company and drove them off the mine known as Chinese Camp, Tuolumne County—a claim which reportedly paid well. Agitation by white miners, themselves immigrants from Europe, against competition from Latin American laborers prompted the California legislature to impose the "Foreign Miners' Tax" of twenty dollars a month in June of 1850. The tax also affected the Chinese.

Miners in front of the Racine Boy Mine in Silver Cliff, Colorado. In Colorado, many Chinese found work in company-owned mines in the Hope Valley and in Denver. Company owners were so pleased with their work that the Colorado legislature passed a joint resolution in 1870, welcoming Chinese laborers to the state, so as to "hasten the development and early prosperity of the Territory."

As surface deposits close to natural waterways became scarce, the miners became more dependent on canal and water companies. Between 1851 and 1852, the changeover from individual to company mining was well under way. For cheap labor, mining companies turned to China, where as early as 1849 a British firm in Shanghai began offering individually contracted Chinese laborers employment in California, along with an advance of $150 in passage money, to be repaid in monthly deductions from their wages. An American consul in Canton reported witnessing the same kind of arrangements in South China in 1849. That year only 325 Chinese arrived in California, based on an estimate by the San Francisco Customs Office. The same office estimated 450 Chinese arrivals in 1850, and 2,700 in 1851. Then, before the end of 1852, over 20,000 Chinese suddenly disembarked in California, coinciding with the beginning of company mining. The event set the stage for continuous agitation by individual white miners determined to evict the Chinese from their midst. The chief objection raised

Chinese Hand Laundry in Delamar, Idaho, c. 1870s. Early Chinese immigrants quickly learned how to find opportunities in the male-inhabited developing communities of the American West. In addition to cooking, they set up hand laundries to provide an essential service that was previously only rarely performed.

(Above) Like other gold prospectors, Chinese miners used the pick-axe, the pan, and the sluice box to work the gravel heaps and tailings of the surface mines. They also used the water wheel, known in America as the "China pump."

(Opposite) "Chinese Quarters, Virginia City, Nevada, 1877." Chinese miners followed the rivers and streams in the Rocky Mountains and settled in the Boise Basin in Idaho, and Helena and Virginia City in Montana. Although cited as Nevada, this may well have been life in the Chinese quarters in Montana.

against the Chinese was that they were willing to work for low wages, although it was couched in other social, religious, political, and economic complaints. The first platform on which the anti-Chinese objections were publicly raised was the notorious Columbia Miners Convention of 1852. It became the prototype of large, well-organized, anti-Chinese movements that would continue for decades to come, in which anti-Chinese and anti-capital sentiments were intrinsically combined. Other incidents of sporadic, uncoordinated anti-Chinese rioting and violence continued to occur throughout the 1850s, 1860s, and 1870s, until they were eventually absorbed into this larger, ideologically defined movement.

By the 1860s, most of the white miners were gone, but the Chinese stayed on and made up almost two-thirds of the mining labor force west of the Rocky Mountains. Typically, they purchased placer mines that were formerly operated by whites, and continued to dig canals and pan the gulches until the last meager returns were squeezed out. From the mines of Mariposa, Placer, and Pine Tree, they moved on to the North Fork of the American River between Jehoval and Cape Horn in California, on to the

Chinese gold miners, California, 1857. Living conditions in the mining camps were primitive and unsanitary.
Chinese miners often slept on the ground, in small tents at the campsite, or huddled together in cabins abandoned by white miners.
They wore the blue cotton tunics and wide-legged trousers typical of menial laborers in China, and combed their hair in pigtails
hanging down their backs, as was demanded of its subjects by the Qing dynasty. A broad-brimmed, pointed hat completed the costume.

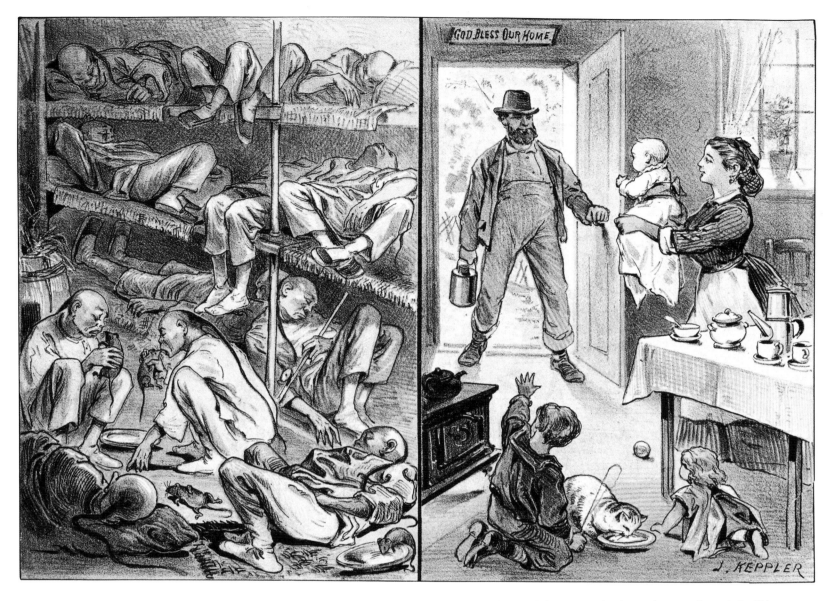

"A Picture for Employers. Why They can live on 40 cents a day, and They can't." Lithograph by J. Keppler in *Puck* magazine, 1878. Chinese men overcome by opium languish on the floor eating rats and sleep cramped several to a bunk-bed in a crowded room, while a husky white worker returns home to a wholesome meal, a smiling wife, and three adorable children. The advent of mining companies employing Chinese laborers set the stage for continuous agitation by individual white miners who wanted to evict the Chinese from their midst. The first objections were raised at the Columbia Miners Convention of 1852, the prototype of all later organized white labor anti-Chinese agitation, which simultaneously targeted employers and Chinese workers.

Rogue and the Umpqua Rivers in southwest Oregon, and up and down the Columbia River and its numerous tributaries in eastern Washington. They were also hired to operate gold and silver mines along the Carson River and Owyhee River, at Silver Peak and in the Red Mountains in Nevada, where, at one time, the entire mining force was Chinese. They founded the town of Dayton in 1855, and in the 1870s there was a Chinese quarter in practically every city in Nevada, including large Chinese communities in Carson City, Reno, Battle Mountain, and Carlin. Following the rivers and streams in the Rocky Mountains, Chinese miners also spread to the Boise Basin in Idaho, to Virginia City and Helena in Montana, and to Deadwood in the Dakota Territories. In 1870, the Colorado legislature passed a joint resolution welcoming Chinese laborers to "hasten the development and early prosperity of the Territory"; there, Chinese found work as employees in company-owned mines in the Hope Valley and Denver. According to the United States census of 1870, more than 11 percent of all miners in the country were Chinese. But in the western states, their percentages were

The only two Chinese hose teams in the United States competed on American Independence Day, July 4, 1888, in the great Hub-to-Hub race held in Deadwood, South Dakota. Chinese miners worked in the gold, silver, copper, coal, salt, borate, and quicksilver mines throughout the western mining states of California, Oregon, Nevada, Washington, Wyoming, Utah, Colorado, Montana, Idaho, and South Dakota.

much more significant: 61.2 percent of the miners in Oregon were from China, 21 percent in Montana, 58.6 percent in Idaho, and in California 25 percent were Chinese. Mining expert Henry Degroot estimated that in 1871 alone Chinese miners extracted and put into circulation over 27 million dollars in gold.

The champion Chinese Hose Team in America, winners of the great Hub-to-Hub race at Deadwood, South Dakota, on July 4, 1888.

Such apparent success did not come easy. Most western states passed discriminatory legislation to protect white miners against competition from the Chinese. The California legislature went the farthest in this respect, although it limited itself to tax legislation. Beginning in 1852, a tax of three dollars was imposed on foreign miners, and employers were made responsible for its payment. In 1853, an amendment raised the tax to four dollars, and tax collectors were authorized to seize the property of those who failed to pay. In 1854, a new law attempting to raise the tax by two dollars at two-year intervals was repealed before it became effective. The state's foreign miners tax receipts steadily grew from 1854 to 1863, but then declined rapidly through 1868; during that period, the Chinese mining population in the state dropped by 68 percent. At the height of the mining taxation

however, the legislature had already extended the mining tax to cover even the Chinese who were not engaged in mining: the Act of 1862 required a monthly payment of $2.50 by each "Mongolian" over the age of eighteen who had not paid the miner's license fee. In addition, to discourage further Chinese immigration, the California Act of 1855 required ship owners to pay $450 for each passenger who was ineligible for citizenship.

Other states restricted the Chinese miners in different ways. The Oregon Constitutional Convention ruled in 1857 that Chinese should not be allowed to own mining claims or land. When Oregon achieved statehood two years later, its legislature levied a five dollar poll tax on every Chinese. In 1864, Washington Territory passed the "Chinese Police Tax"—a special quarterly six dollar capitation tax levied on every "Mongolian" in the territory. The sheriff in each county was entitled to keep 25 percent of the money he collected. In addition, the Chinese were prohibited from giving court testimony in any disputes involving whites. Similar rules were in effect in Montana, Nevada, and Idaho.

Such legal discrimination no doubt further encouraged white miners' contempt for and violence against the Chinese. The Chinese resisted as best they could. Eventually, the discriminatory laws were declared unconstitutional by state or federal courts. In 1871, the United States commissioner for the collection of mining statistics concluded that the presence of Chinese miners in this country was in fact desirable and that Chinese labor would come to be valued not for its economy but for its excellence. Many

Hanging in large wicker baskets that were suspended by pulleys, Chinese railroad workers risked their lives to set dynamite charges to blast through the mountains. They devised this unique method in the spring of 1866, during construction of the Central Pacific Railroad, while assaulting the cliffs of Cape Horn Mountain, which rose two thousand feet above the base of the American River Canyon. Between 12,000 and 14,000 Chinese were employed on the construction, and over twelve hundred of them perished during the project—almost one in ten.

employers shared this view and hired Chinese to work in salt basins around San Francisco Bay, to mine borate deposits in Oregon, Nevada, and California, coal in Washington, Wyoming, and Utah, and quicksilver in California's Napa and Lake counties.

RAILROADS

As mentioned earlier, the Central Pacific Railway Company also decided to draw on the Chinese labor supply when it was chartered by a Congressional Act of 1862 to build the first American transcontinental railroad along with the Union Pacific. The Central Pacific had a more formidable task because it had to cross the Sierra Nevada—a solid wall of granite—and the arid plains and deserts of Nevada and Utah on its eastward drive from Sacramento. As the two companies raced for federal subsidies, cheaper Chinese labor seemed to be the answer for the Central Pacific. While a white worker was paid on the average thirty-five dollars a month plus room and board, a Chinese laborer received between twenty-six and thirty-five dollars a month and had to provide his own food and

Chinese laborers at work with wheelbarrows and one-horse dump-carts on the Southern Pacific Railroad lines of Sacramento, California, in 1877. Between 1868 and 1883, many Chinese were hired to work on a variety of major rail projects in the southern and southwestern United States, for the Houston-Texas Central Railway Company, the Alabama-Chattanooga Railroad, and the Southern Pacific.

Joseph Becker. *Snow Sheds on the Central Pacific Railroad in the Sierra Nevada Mountains.* **Oil on canvas. 19 x 26 in. Collection of the Gilcrease Museum, Tulsa, OK. The problem of harsh winter weather creating life-threatening conditions for the railroad workers laying tracks across the mountains was met by the construction of snow sheds. It was the Chinese who laid the tracks and built the snow sheds. Many were killed by avalanches, and remained buried under snow until it melted in the spring.**

lodging. Before the completion of the railroad, between twelve thousand and fourteen thousand Chinese were on the Central Pacific payroll. They leveled the roadbeds, dug the tunnels, and blasted the mountains. In the spring of 1866, when assaulting Cape Horn Mountain, they devised an ingenious solution to a difficult tunneling problem. They used reeds to weave large wicker baskets, which they then lowered by a pulley system over cliffs two thousand feet above the base of the American River Canyon. Each basket held two workers, who chiseled holes through the granite escarpments, placed the dynamite in them, and lit it, before being pulled up to the top of the cliff just in time to escape the explosion. Needless to say, accidents were frequent. The difficult work was made even more dangerous by the severe winter weather of the High Sierra. Many who were covered by snow slides were not found until the following spring when the snow melted. It was estimated that more than twelve hundred Chinese perished during the project—almost one in ten. And although Leland Stanford, president of the Central Pacific, highly praised his Chinese employees, when the formal junction of the two railroads took place in 1869 at Promontory Point, Utah, the Chinese were not allowed to take part in the festivities.

Nevertheless, the news of the competence and effectiveness of Chinese laborers quickly spread, and between 1868 and 1883 they appeared as construction workers on a variety of other major rail projects, including the Canadian Pacific. They were employed by the Northern Pacific Railway Company and the Oregon Railway and Navigation Company to lay tracks and telegraph lines throughout Oregon, Washington, Idaho, and Montana. They were signed up by the Houston-Texas Central Railway Company in 1869 and traveled to Houston via Council Bluffs, Iowa; St. Louis; and New

Chinese workers, riding the rails along Clark Fork river, Montana, in August 1890. During the 1880s, the Northern Pacific imported 15,000 workers from China to build the first northern transcontinental line—Chinese workers outnumbered white workers by three to two.

A Chinese cook and his employers on the porch of the engineer's office on Poso Ranch, Kern County, California, in 1888. Many Chinese found work providing food and services to the mining crews, railroad workers, loggers, and field workers throughout the fast-developing western and southwestern United States.

Orleans. They worked on the Alabama-Chattanooga railroad in 1870, and on the Southern Pacific, which connected San Francisco with El Paso, Texas, in 1881, by running south through California and east across Arizona, New Mexico, and Texas.

FOOD AND SERVICES

After the construction of the railroads was completed, most of the discharged workers remained in the areas the railroads had taken them to and looked for other kinds of work. In the Northwest region, where railroad construction had stimulated the development of the lumber industry, a substantial number of Chinese found employment cleaning sawmills, store-keeping, cooking, and performing other logging-related jobs. They opened a number of general stores in Portland and Seattle, and settled in smaller communities in Rock Springs and Evanston, Wyoming, and Brigham City, Park City, and Scofield, Utah. In the Southwest, they established Chinese enclaves in Phoenix, Tucson, Tempe, Albuquerque, El Paso, and San Antonio, where they set themselves to work as laundrymen, cooks, barbers, servants, grocers, and truck gardeners.

As they often did later, when faced with discrimination and exclusion, the Chinese showed great resourcefulness in finding untapped job opportunities. At first they provided food and services to the mining crews. Next, they were growing food and cooking for the railroad workers. Before long, they were cooking for loggers and field workers. Thanks to their effort and skill in growing vegetables, the diet and health of a typical resident of American West was greatly improved. As word of their food cultivation and production skills spread, and as their reputation for being "quiet, peaceable, patient, industrious and economical" grew, the Chinese soon became employed as cooks, stewards, and gardeners in wealthy households. In his later years, James Beard, one of the most influential food writers of the twentieth century, recalled his boyhood in Oregon and wrote admiringly of his mother's Chinese cook, Let. He cited many of Let's recipes in his memoirs. Little by little, Chinese cooking made steady inroads into American culture.

Chinese workers in a California vineyard. In the 1870s, as much as three-quarters of the agricultural work in California was performed by Chinese laborers.

AGRICULTURE

(Opposite) **A Chinese resident of Idaho City, Idaho, who grew and peddled his own vegetables, contributing to the increasingly healthy diet of the residents.**

Perhaps the biggest but least recognized contribution of the Chinese in the New World was in agriculture. In 1876, California's wheat growers testified to a special Congressional committee that without Chinese labor they could not raise wheat and bring it to market, and that their entire crop would have failed had the Chinese not been there for the harvest. Then, when the transcontinental railroad gave California's farmers easier access to East Coast markets, and they began to grow more profitable fruits and vegetables, they employed the Chinese to do the planting, pruning, grafting, and harvesting of these labor-intensive crops. Chinese settlements emerged throughout the state of California, with particularly large ones in Santa Clara, Fresno, Sacramento, and Alameda counties. Between 1870 and 1882, Chinese laborers performed an estimated two-thirds to nine-tenths of all agricultural work in California. Even in 1890, as California drew an ever-increasing number of white settlers, an estimated 20 percent of the state's agricultural workforce was still Chinese.

It is largely due to the toil of Chinese laborers who worked in waist-deep water to dam sloughs, cut drainage ditches, and build floodgates and levees that the thousands of acres of swamps in the Sacramento-San Joaquin Delta became the fertile and productive land that it is today. After the land recla-mation projects were completed, many of the Chinese who had worked on them stayed to work in the fruit orchards along the Sacramento River banks. Others were employed to cultivate sugar beets and hops, and some managed to lease ranches and become truck-gardeners selling sweet pota-toes and vegetables. But during the 1890s their numbers began to decline, and today only the town of Locke still survives—the last concentration of Chinese in rural California. It is the only town in the United States built exclusively by the Chinese for the Chinese.

Other areas of the United States also benefited from Chinese agricultural labor during the last quarter of the nineteenth century, most notably the Pacific Northwest and the deep South, where the Chinese were used to tend orchards, build canals, pick cotton, and harvest rice. But they

The Chinese Mission School in Monterey, California, serving the Chinese fishing community, c. 1885–1900.

did more than just provide muscle power; they were also instrumental in introducing new varieties of plants and hybrids previously unknown in America. They pioneered new varieties of rice, and turned celery into a commercial crop. Indeed, Chinese farmers are responsible for influencing the American way of life in many subtle, yet pervasive ways. How many Americans are aware that they owe their morning glass of cheap orange juice to Lue Gim Gong of De Land Florida, who in 1888 developed the frost-resistant orange, which made possible the great citrus industry of that state? How many know that the most famous variety of cherry—the "Bing cherry"—bears the name of Chinese horticultural expert Ah Bing, who worked for several years in Milwaukie, Oregon, and who is responsible for introducing the hybrid cherry tree to the Pacific Northwest?

FISHING

In the 1850s, Chinese were among the first settlers of the West Coast to engage in commercial fishing. They did so by using mesh nets and hooks and vessels familiar to them at home: wooden sampans for gathering and large junks for transporting their catch. Chinese fishing activities steadily grew throughout the 1860s in California. They established several fishing villages at Humboldt Bay and at what is now Marine Laboratory Point near Pacific Grove. By 1870, their activities encompassed the entire Pacific coast of the United States, with major centers in San Diego, Monterey, and San Francisco.

The Chinese fished, gathered, processed, and marketed a wide variety of marine life. They fished salmon, crab, squid, sturgeon, and other·fish found both in the ocean bays and rivers on the coast. Starting in the 1860s, and on through the 1870s and 1880s, many caught sharks off Santa Catalina for a living. The sharks' commercial value lay in its fins—a high-priced delicacy in Chinese cuisine—and in its liver, which was processed into a lubricating oil. Abalone was another sea creature introduced to the commercial market by the Chinese. Its meat was marketed in the Far East, where it has long been regarded as a precious food commodity, while its shells found their way to the East Coast and Europe, where they were used as raw material for jewelry. Seaweed, gathered off the rocky shores of the Monterey peninsula, once dried and processed, was another rare delicacy with high market value in Asia.

Chinese fishermen and their boats at Point Alones Village on Monterey peninsula, California, in 1895. The presence of many children indicates that the Chinese fishermen had settled in California with the intention to stay.

In the 1870s and 1880s, their expertise in drying and packing seafood got many Chinese jobs in the new shrimp industry in California and Louisiana. They were also employed in the salmon canneries that were springing up all along the Pacific Northwest coast, from Oregon and Washington to British Columbia and Alaska. In the late 1870s, nearly 80 percent of all the cannery workers on the Columbia River were Chinese.

Once again, Chinese hard work and expertise posed a threat to white competitors. Bowing to white pressure, legislators passed laws to curtail Chinese fishing activities, from a discriminatory tax of four dollars a month imposed in 1860 on every Chinese fisherman to the restrictions of the use of mesh nets, and limitations on the shrimp fishing season. Finally, in 1905, the exportation of dried shrimp from California was banned. Due to the hostile legal environment, which saw the sinking of Chinese boats and the slashing of their nets, by 1900 the once vibrant Chinese fishing community was reduced to just a few decaying fishing camps.

OTHER INDUSTRIES

After the railroad and mining jobs dried up, Chinese scattered all across the West Coast to assume a variety of industrial jobs. As mentioned earlier, they were recruited in 1870 to replace the striking white workers in Calvin T. Sampson's shoe factories in North Adams, Massachusetts; in Passaic Steam Laundry in Belleville, New Jersey; and in the Beaver Falls Cutlery Company in Beaver Falls, Pennsylvania. Employers went on hiring Chinese instead of raising the white workers' wages; by 1873 over 50 percent of the shoes and boots made in California were manufactured by Chinese.

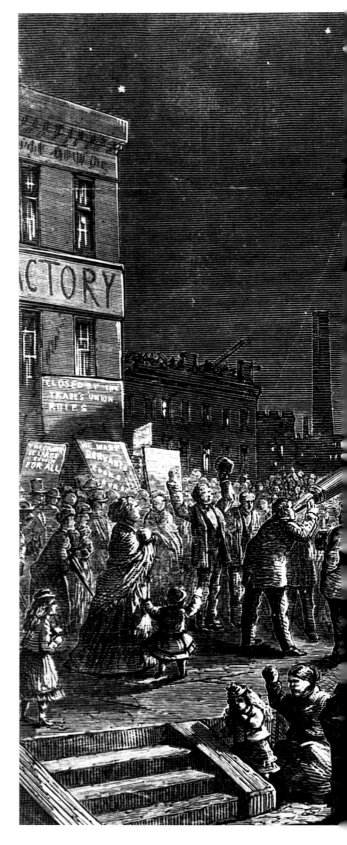

"The New Comet—A Phenomenon Now Visible in All Parts of the United States." Drawing by Thomas Nast, well-known political cartoonist, from *Harper's Weekly*, 1870. The whole nation aims its telescope lenses at the flying comet with Chinese features called "Cheap Labor." In every endeavor where they competed with white workers, the Chinese provoked the ire of organized white labor. White labor unions, unwilling to accept and organize Chinese laborers, pressured the California legislature to adopt discriminatory taxes that specifically targeted the Chinese in all major industries. The popular press often picked up the anti-capital, anti-Chinese stance.

Chinese also competed with white workers in the woolen industry. They were among the first workers to be hired by Heyneman, Pick and Company of San Francisco, and among the last to be fired when economic recession and then depression set in after 1867, because they didn't demand higher wages. The same was true in the sewing and clothing industries, causing great anger among white workers whose labor movement eventually turned violent against the Chinese.

The only environment where Chinese industrial workers could work without racial tension was the Chinese-owned cigar factory. Since they didn't require much start-up capital, during the 1860s and 1870s between sixty and seventy Chinese merchants were active in cigar manufacturing, accounting for two-thirds of the San Francisco cigar revenue stamps sold by the Bureau of Internal Revenue. The Chinese cigar workers even formed a labor union called the Tang Dak Tong, or Hall of Common Virtue, which protected their wages and their working environment from non-union members. Sadly, the Chinese cigar union was not recognized by the white Cigar Makers Union of California, which only goes to show that white workers' racial prejudices overrode what should have been their common class interests.

Finally, many Chinese found work as seamen, firemen, coal passers, stewards, cooks, cabin boys, storekeepers, bakers, porters, pantrymen, waiters, and boatswains on the Occidental and Oriental Steamship Company and the Pacific Mail Steamship Company ships. The steamships which traded between San Francisco and Asian ports used only Chinese as deckhands and helpers in their engineer and steward departments. Between 1876 and 1906, a total of 78,433 Chinese worked in such capacities on American ships. Eighty-eight Chinese seamen were even used aboard Admiral George Dewey's Pacific fleet during the Spanish-American War, but due to the restrictive immigration laws targeting Chinese, they were not allowed to participate in the hero's welcome parade in San Francisco, although they had been invited by the Admiral.

"A Word of Caution to Our Friends, the Cigar-Makers. Through the smoke it is easy to see the approach of Chinese cheap labor." Cartoon. 1877.
A warning to cigar makers not to use Chinese labor. Trade unions, fearful of competing with cheap Chinese labor,
supported restrictions against Chinese immigration during the 1870s and 1880s.

A CLOSER LOOK:
CHANG AND ENG

In 1829 two 18-year-old Chinese boys, Chang and Eng, arrived at Boston on the U.S. ship *Sachem*. They instantly attracted wide attention among physicians and the general public, because they were twins, joined at the chest by a thick, muscular ligament. Since they were born in Siam (now Thailand), they became known as the "Siamese Twins"—a name henceforth applied to all physically united twins. The young men, having been "discovered" by British merchant Robert Hunter, were initially treated as freaks, and they toured with carnivals in the United States and Europe between 1829 and 1854. But, despite their condition, they managed to lead long and productive lives. They amassed a fortune of $60,000, married two North Carolina women, Sarah and Adelaide (born Yates), and sired 22 children between them. Chang was even called on to serve their adopted country during the Civil War—and would have done so but for the shock of the commanding officer when the two showed up. Several of their sons served instead.

(Above) **Chang and Eng Bunker (1811–74)**
and *(right)* **with their wives and children (c. 1853).**

CHINESE EXCLUSION

The Chinese were not welcomed as equals in America, even though their labor was eagerly sought by American employers. The 1868 Burlingame Treaty with China gave the Chinese the right of unlimited immigration into the United States. But in the eyes of other Americans, the Chinese were merely the cheapest form of labor available after the abolition of slavery. Since in many cases they replaced black slaves, their poor treatment, no doubt, was owed in part to that fact. As people of color, the Chinese were automatically seen as inferior, unassimilable aliens.

It did not help that the Chinese came from a backward country where visiting Westerners found no recognizable religious beliefs. Christian religious groups referred to them as heathens—morally inferior people without free will, to whom the Western tradition of democratic thinking was entirely alien, and who were thus willing to tolerate abuses by autocrats and bullies. Such perceptions were freely circulated at the time, in publications like *Puck, Harper's Weekly: A Journal of Civilization, Frank Leslie's Illustrated Newspaper,* and *The San Francisco Illustrated Wasp,* known for their harsh indictments of each new immigrant group to arrive on U.S. shores. The Chinese fared as badly as, if not worse than, other ethnic groups. In its January 30, 1858, issue, for example, the *Harper's Weekly* carried a cartoon of three "Celestial Ladies" with a caption that read, "The taste for the baboon-like faces of Hong Kong women is, I fancy, like that for mangoes, an

(Previous spread) Chinese immigrants being searched for opium in San Francisco, California, 1882. After the passage of the Chinese Exclusion Act in 1882, Chinese immigrants were subjected to physical searches, rigorous interrogation, and intimidation by immigration officials, who, no doubt, thought they were merely upholding the law.

(Opposite) An Uncle Sam figure kicks Chinese hand-launderers off the scene in a poster advertising a new product—"The Magic Washer." During the early days of the Gold Rush, many lodging establishments in San Francisco sent their laundry by ship to Hawaii for washing. Chinese immigrants jumped at the opportunity to provide this indispensable service.

"Celestial Ladies." *Harper's Weekly,* January 30, 1858. Chinese women, no exception to the commonly held view that nonwhite races were inferior, were harshly caricatured as having "baboon-like faces" in the publications of the times.

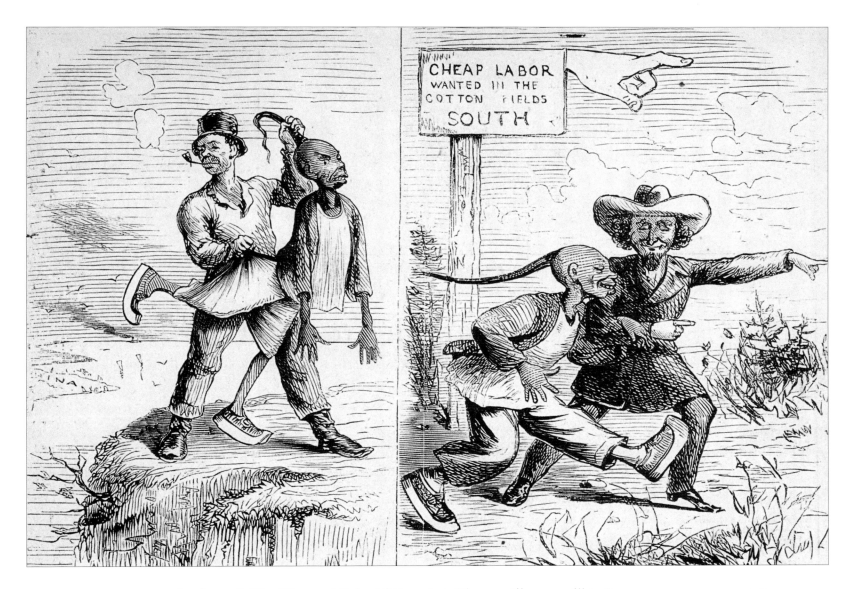

acquired one." *The Wasp* published "Darwin's Theory Illustrated" in January 1877, presenting what it called "The Creation of Chinaman and Pig."

"The Nigger Must Go, the Chinaman Must Go," cried *Harper's Weekly* in January 1879, echoing the position of organized white labor. *The San Francisco Illustrated Wasp* dealt "The First Blow at the Chinese Question" on December 8, 1877, with a picture of a white worker carrying a Workingmen's Procession placard and punching a Chinese in the nose. And, in a double-twisted irony, the Chinese were both urged to leave the United States and never come back, and reproached for the lack of loyalty and commitment to the country where they "stole jobs." Under such pressure many did end up wanting to leave as soon as they made enough money to do so. This relegated them to the category of mere "sojourners" in the eyes of their white fellow immigrants—a term used to imply that they had no desire to settle in the United States—although their migration followed a similar pattern to that of Europeans.

"What Shall We Do with John Chinaman?" *Frank Leslie's Illustrated Newspaper,* September 25, 1869. Pat sends the poor Chinese packing down south to the cotton fields, showing where the Chinese belonged in the eyes of the Irish immigrants.

The booming mining towns and railroad camps of the West were notoriously "male societies, " populated by adventuresome, strong, and usually
poor single young men, who were trying to make a quick buck before
"returning to civilization" to marry. Very few women ever set foot there.
The Chinese were no exception. The contracted Chinese laborers were
expected to return to China after they made their fortune in the New
World. Or, if they were to discover that the Gold Mountain offered good
prospects for stable family life, the women would follow them there when
the conditions were right. Consequently, there were only seven Chinese
women in San Francisco in 1850, among 4,018 men, and only 1,784 in
1860, when the great demand for Chinese male labor raised the number of
men to 33,149 in the city alone. The Chinese society on the Gold
Mountain was without a doubt a male one.

It should not come as a surprise that the Gold Rush communities in
California provided fertile ground for the flourishing of the world's oldest
trade: prostitution. In this respect, too, Chinese were no different from the

**"There are none so
Blind as Those Who
Won't See."** A newly
arrived group of
Chinese immigrants
read signs announcing
job opportunities. The
economic and social
decline that imperial
China experienced
during the second half
of the 19th century
created the "push
factor" in Chinese emi-
gration. The "pull"
was provided by the
United States employ-
ers in need of cheap
and subservient labor-
ers after the abolition
of slavery. Able-bodied
men were recruited
in southern coastal
China under a "credit
ticket" system, which
gave them deferred-
payment sea passage.
Their transportation
debts forced them to
accept jobs at any pay
they could get, and
often forced them to
work in conditions of
indentured servitude.

"The First Blow at the Chinese Question." *The Wasp*, December 8, 1877. This first anti-Chinese cartoon published in *The Wasp* clearly shows the white laborer's hostility toward the Chinese workers who would deprive them of their jobs.

other miners. The only difference was that most white prostitutes came to California as independent professionals or worked in brothels for wages, while the Chinese prostitutes were typically imported as indentured servants after they had been sold in China by their poor parents for $70 to $150, or lured and kidnapped by procurers, and then resold in the United States for $350 to $1,000 or more. One notable exception was a woman called Ah Toy, who arrived by herself in San Francisco in 1849 from Hong Kong to "better her condition." She soon became the first and most successful Chinese courtesan in the city, her entrepreneurship well known in the city's courtroom and newsrooms. Reports of the time recorded that

A Slave Girl in Holiday Attire, Chinatown, San Francisco. c. 1896–1906. Photo by Arnold Genthe. Due to the prohibition of sexual relations between white women and Chinese men, and the ratio of twenty-seven men to one woman among Chinese immigrants in California, the demand for Chinese prostitutes was huge. Girls were often bought from poor families or kidnapped in China, and resold by procurers to brothels in the United States to work as indentured servants, or, practically, slaves.

men paid an ounce of gold and lined up around the block just to "gaze upon the countenance of the charming Ah Toy."

The demand for Chinese prostitutes was huge in California because of the prohibition of sexual relations between white women and Chinese men, and because of the shortage of Chinese women—both conditions that also made it impossible for Chinese men to marry and raise families. An estimated 85 percent of the 1,784 Chinese women in San Francisco in 1860 were prostitutes. (The number dropped to 71 percent in 1870, and went down further to 21 percent in 1880.) The trafficking in Chinese prostitutes became a lucrative trade, with immigration officials, policemen, and white Chinatown property owners who rented to brothels profiting handsomely in the process. But the biggest winner was the secret society, the Hip Yee Tong, which reportedly netted $200,000 between 1852 and 1873. Competing groups, known as *tongs,* after the Chinese word for chamber or meeting place, began to fight over the control of this profitable business, and the violent tong wars that erupted during the 1870s and 1880s received great attention in the press. The Chinese, previously vilified as backward, defiled, and infidel, now received sensationalized treatment as bloodthirsty gangsters, gamblers, and pimps.

Methodist and Presbyterian missionaries jumped to the rescue of Chinese prostitutes in 1874, using extensive press coverage of their police-assisted raids on Chinese brothels to turn public opinion against Chinese prostitution. A number of established institutions added their weight to the issue, and in 1875, the Forty-third U.S. Congress passed an act that prohibited immigration of "any subject of China, Japan, or any Oriental country . . . for lewd and immoral purposes," forbade the importation of prostitutes, and authorized immigration officers to board incoming vessels and inspect them for prostitutes and convicts. Although the intentions of Christian missionaries may have been noble, the offshoot of the anti-prostitution act, known as the Page Law, was that the American public began to view all Chinese women as prostitutes. Also, many wives left behind in China were discouraged from coming to the United States to join their husbands because they knew that they would be subjected to rigorous cross-exami-

"The Anti-Chinese Wall: The American Wall Goes Up as the Chinese Original Goes Down." *Puck,* **March 29, 1882. As the Great Wall of China is broken down, allowing merchants and missionaries to enter, a wall of prejudice, jealousy, and non-reciprocity is built up by American laborers to keep the Chinese out.**

nation and intimidation. During the seven years after the enactment of the Page Law, the number of Chinese women entering the United States dropped by 68 percent compared to the previous seven years. Later, with the introduction of the 1882 Chinese Exclusion Act, all working-class women were rejected on account of being "laborers."

With the passage of such discriminatory laws, Chinese immigration to the United States was curbed to the point that even the usually hostile *Puck* magazine took a compassionate look at the Chinese in December 1900. "But why is it," asked a thoughtful Chinese on its cover page, "that I may go to your heaven, while I may not go to your country?" The American missionary shrugged his shoulders. "There is no Labor vote in heaven!" said he.

THE 1882 CHINESE EXCLUSION ACT

The anti-Chinese attacks and political agitation started in California and were at first confined to the West Coast, where the white workers refused to work alongside Chinese. During the 1860s, white workers staged protests and forced the passage of numerous municipal and state tax laws and harass-

The anti-Chinese riot that occurred in Denver, Colorado, on November 20, 1880, was just one of many incidents of racial violence that plagued Chinese communities in American Western states, particularly during the decade leading up to the Chinese Exclusion Act of 1882. Typically, a mob of white men found a minor pretext to rampage through Chinatown, burn or destroy homes and businesses, and attack the residents.

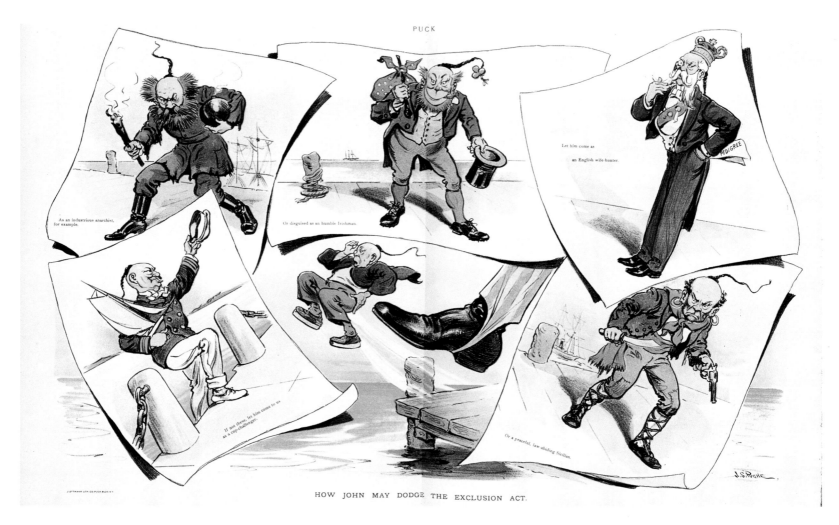

PUCK

HOW JOHN MAY DODGE THE EXCLUSION ACT.

"How John May Dodge the Exclusion Act," *Puck*, July 12, 1905. "As an English wife-hunter," "disguised as an humble Irishman," just two of the six ways anti-Chinese paranoia was reflected in the popular press, with suggestions on how Chinese might try to sneak into the country after the harsh Chinese Exclusion Act of 1882.

ment laws, aimed specifically at the Chinese, in order to make their life in the United States difficult. They also organized street riots against Chinese laborers in San Francisco in the summer of 1869. Pressure to exclude Chinese labor from California continued to rise throughout the 1870s, but since the Civil Rights Act of 1870 prohibited discrimination against any person and barred the imposition of immigration taxes on any particular group of nonresidents, the Chinese were for a time able to challenge and strike down in federal courts the discriminatory state and municipal laws that specifically targeted them.

Despite such legal setbacks, white workers and independent farmers continued to agitate against them. The anti-Chinese forces would not be defeated by federal courts; their agitation simply took on a more organized, political form. They mounted countrywide campaigns calling for the repeal of the Burlingame Treaty. Opportunistic politicians used the anti-Chinese issue to advance their own standing. The Democratic Party, in decline since the Civil War on account of its pro-slavery position, staged a successful comeback in California and elsewhere after 1870, largely on a platform that featured attacks on Chinese labor and immigration. The Republican Party

"The Ultimate Cause." *Puck,* December 19, 1900. A spoof of the American double-standards through an imaginary dialogue between an American missionary to China and a would-be Chinese immigrant. "But why is it," asked the thoughtful Chinese, "that I may go to your heaven, while I may not go to your country?" The American missionary shrugged his shoulders. "There is no Labor vote in heaven!" said he.

followed suit, to cash in on the popular anti-Chinese sentiment. Trade-union organizers capitalized on the sentiment, too, to rally skilled white workers. "Anti-coolie clubs" sprung up throughout the state of California, organized by the local politicians and union leaders.

Such an openly hostile, racist climate led to a race riot at Los Angeles in the summer of 1871, which left nineteen Chinese dead from shooting, hanging, and stabbing, and many more injured. By 1876, when the Hayes-Tilden compromise effectively ended the Reconstruction era, the practices of racial segregation and discrimination known as Jim Crowism, which had at first been directed against the freed black slaves, began to affect the Chinese as well. The California legislature appointed a special committee to investigate the social, moral, and political effects of Chinese immigration, and while the committee held its hearings, the anti-Chinese "lobby" organized a mass rally in the Union Hall in San Francisco, forcing a resolution that demanded an end to Chinese immigration. As a result, hostilities toward the Chinese grew even more rampant. When, in July of 1877, a San Francisco mob burned down twenty-five Chinatown laundries, setting off anti-Chinese riots that lasted for months, the Chinese received little or no police protection. Their predicament gave rise to the phrase "not a Chinaman's chance." In 1878, the state legislature passed a law prohibiting persons barred from citizenship (all Asians not born in America) from owning land. In 1879, that law was incorporated into California's new constitution, which also prohibited employment of Chinese by any state, county, or municipal office "except in punishment for a crime," and specified that no corporation formed under state law was allowed to employ, directly or indirectly, any Chinese or Mongolian.

Such direct efforts to force Chinese out of California through local legislation were threatened by judges who insisted on upholding equal rights for Chinese under the Constitution of the United States and laws passed by the Congress, and so the "disruptive issue" was brought to Washington, D.C., in 1878 for treatment by the Congress. China's first minister to the United States lobbied for the cause of Chinese in America, prompting President Rutherford B. Hayes in 1879 to veto the first bill that would have limited

No. 6297   **DUPLICATE.**

UNITED STATES OF AMERICA.

Certificate of Residence.

Issued to Chinese _____ LABORER _____, under the Provisions of the Act of May 5, 1892.

This is to Certify THAT *Sam Lee* _____, a Chinese _____ LABORER _____, now residing at CHICAGO.

has made application No. 697 to me for a Certificate of Residence, under the provisions of the Act of Congress approved May 5, 1892, and I certify that it appears, from the affidavits of witnesses submitted with said application that said *Sam Lee* was within the limits of the United States at the time of the passage of said Act, and was then residing at *Chicago Ills* and that he was at that time lawfully entitled to remain in the United States, and that the following is a descriptive list of said Chinese LABORER viz.:

NAME: *Sam Lee*   AGE: *35*

LOCAL RESIDENCE: *299 W. Lake St* CHICAGO

OCCUPATION: *Laundryman* HEIGHT: *5ft 4* COLOR OF EYES: DARK BROWN

COMPLEXION: *Dark*   PHYSICAL MARKS OR PECULIARITIES FOR

IDENTIFICATION: *Scar on each side of Mouth*

And as a further means of identification I have affixed hereto a photographic likeness of said *Sam Lee*.

GIVEN UNDER MY HAND AND SEAL this *3rd* day of *April*, 189*4*, at CHICAGO. State of ILLINOIS

[SEAL]

W. J. Mize
Collector of Internal Revenue,
District of _____

2—1498

immigration from China to fifteen individuals coming in on any given ship at one time. President Hays, fearing that the bill might endanger America's trade with China, quoted violation of the Burlingame Treaty as the grounds for his veto. The supporters of anti-Chinese legislation then instructed American diplomats to seek a revision of the treaty, which had just some dozen years earlier been forced on China. After unexpected resistance from the Chinese government, terms of a new treaty were agreed on late in 1880. The new treaty allowed that the United States government had the right to "regulate, limit or suspend, . . . but not absolutely prohibit" the coming of "Chinese laborers." On the other hand, it also stipulated that "Chinese subjects, whether proceeding to the United States as teachers, students, merchants, or from curiosity, together with their body and household servants, and Chinese laborers now in the United States shall be allowed to come and go of their own free will and accord, and shall be accorded all

A certificate of residence issued in 1892 to a Chinese laborer, Chicago. Chinese who were already in the U.S. in 1882 were allowed to stay on as residents, without citizenship and no guarantee of re-entry if they left the country.

(Opposite) **"The Chinese Question."** *Harper's Weekly,* **February 18, 1871, from a drawing by Thomas Nast. Amidst widespread agitation against Chinese labor and cries of "Chinamen must go!" this magazine raised its voice in support of the basic principles of American democracy. While "Miss Columbia" protects the Chinese from an angry mob, the issues inscribed on the wall in this 1871 cartoon sum up the prejudices and fears of white laborers that culminated in the 1882 Chinese Exclusion Act.**

the rights, privileges, immunities, and exemptions which are accorded to the citizens and subjects of the most favored nation." The treaty was formally ratified in October 1881. It untied the hands of the Congress in dealing with "the matter of Chinese immigration."

When the Forty-seventh Congress of the United States convened in 1882, the senator from California introduced a new bill to suspend the immigration of Chinese laborers. By this time the issue of Chinese exclusion had grown into a national movement, and the bill received support from the representatives of all Western states and most of the Southern Democrats. The bill generated a great deal of debate between the executive branch of the U.S. government and the Congress. Shortly after it passed the Congress, it was vetoed by President Chester A. Arthur, who objected to some of its stipulations on the ground that they violated the most-favored-nation guarantee and were likely to drive Asian trade away and cause ill feeling toward the United States. A new bill was immediately drawn to address the President's objections, and on May 6, 1882, President Arthur signed the precedent-setting bill into law. Known as the Chinese Exclusion Act, it was the first and only federal law in the history of the United States to exclude a group of people on the basis of ethnic origin. The only previous federal exclusion act, passed in 1875, was designed to keep out prostitutes and criminals other than political prisoners. Another law, enacted later in 1882, excluded convicts, lunatics, idiots, and any person who was liable to become a public charge. Since the 1882 Chinese Exclusion Act, Congress has been careful to refrain from using racial, national, or ethnic distinctions as grounds for exclusion. Nevertheless, the uniquely scornful treatment accorded the Chinese by the nation's highest law-making body remains a dark mark on its record.

THE RISE OF
CHINESE GHETTOS

Not only was the entry of Chinese laborers, both skilled and unskilled, into the United States suspended; state and federal courts were not allowed to naturalize the Chinese who were already in the country. The Chinese residing in the United States were not allowed to bring their wives into the country; nor were they assured of re-entry themselves if they were to visit China and return. And, as if to ensure their complete biological extinction, they were barred from marrying whites by the racist miscegenation laws, which were only finally declared unconstitutional by the U.S. Supreme Court in 1967. The harsh exclusion laws were meant to eliminate the Chinese from the United States in one generation.

Violent attacks against the Chinese intensified after the passage of the Exclusion Act. The anti-Chinese forces unleashed an "abatement" campaign to drive them out of the mines, ships, and lumber camps by force. Chinese were harassed or expelled from thirty-four communities in California, nine in the state of Washington, three in Oregon, and four in Nevada. In the mining towns of Colorado, Alaska, and South Dakota, millions of dollars worth of Chinese property was damaged and burned. The worst incidents occurred in Eureka (1885), Redlands (1893), and Chico (1894) in California; and in Juneau, Alaska (1886). On September 2, 1885, some 150 white employees of the Rock Springs mines in Wyoming

(Opposite) The Street of the Gamblers (by day). **c. 1895–1906. Photo by Arnold Genthe, from his series of photographs of San Francisco's Old Chinatown. Isolated and locked in their own ways, the Chinatowns that sprang up after the anti-Chinese mob violence of the 1880s came to represent a different, mysterious world in the eyes of outside observers and their camera lenses. Arnold Genthe—the most famous photo-chronicler of San Francisco's Chinatown at the turn of the century— did not shy away from tampering with his photographs for greater "mystery effect."**

suddenly attacked their 331 Chinese co-workers, killing twenty-eight, wounding fifteen, and chasing several hundred out of town. When Wyoming authorities attempted to investigate the massacre, witnesses were intimidated and the grand jury brought no indictments.

The Wyoming Massacre, September 2, 1888. **Anti-Chinese hysteria and violence peaked in the year 1885. The most horrifying atrocities occurred in the mountain states and the Northwest. Because of the fear of recrimination, there was no legal action taken against any members of the mob that attacked Chinese co-workers in the Rock Springs mines in 1885.**

This seems to have emboldened the anti-Chinese agitators in the coal mines of Washington Territory. On September 11, 1885, the Chinese settlement of coal miners at Coal Creek was burned down. Eight days later Chinese miners were driven out of the Black Diamond area. Nine of them were seriously injured. On September 28, anti-Chinese activists organized an "Anti-Chinese Congress" in Seattle, to frighten the Chinese there. Then, on the night of October 24, 1885, the Chinese community in Seattle was burned down. On November 3, a mob of three hundred men in Tacoma forced all Chinese residents to leave their homes. After the success in Tacoma, the mob went to the smaller towns of Pierce, King, Kitsap, Snohomish, Skagit, and Whatcom, and expelled all the Chinese there as well. Their proclamation demanded that all Chinese leave Washington

Anti-Chinese riot in Seattle, Washington Territory, 1886. *Harper's Weekly,* March 6, 1886. In Washington Territory, many Chinese miners and hop-pickers were murdered. The entire population of Tacoma was packed into boxcars and sent to Portland. Anti-Chinese rioters in Seattle organized an "Anti-Chinese Congress" on September 28, 1855, and, on the night of October 24, burned down the Chinese community. In November, they threatened to shed blood if the whole Chinese population of Washington Territory did not leave within a day.

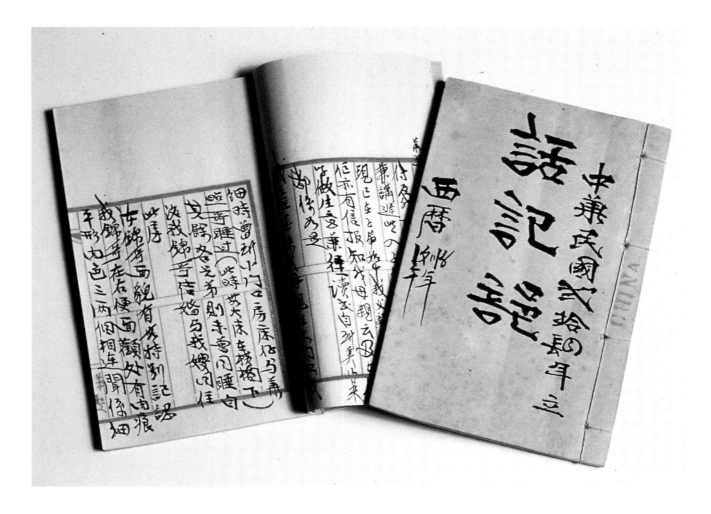

The children of U.S. citizens were allowed to enter the country legally, but some Chinese managed to beat the immigration restrictions by bringing over "paper sons," who learned the "appropriate" family history from "coaching books," such as this one. Such books were frequently studied enroute to the U.S. and thrown overboard or destroyed as the ship approached American shores.

Territory within a day lest they all be evicted. On November 7, President Grover Cleveland sent federal troops into Tacoma and Seattle to restore law and order. The riots were finally suppressed by noon on November 8.

The objective of anti-Chinese mob violence in 1885 was to drive the Chinese out of white communities. To protect themselves, the Chinese were forced to take up residence in ethnic concentrations in major metropolitan areas—first on the West Coast, and later in New York, Philadelphia, Cleveland, Boston, Chicago, Washington, and other cities— which gave rise to the now ubiquitous fixture of urban America: the Chinatown. Since white workers typically refused to work alongside Chinese workers, and since very few white employers would risk the ire of the organized and militant white labor unions by employing the Chinese, the Chinese were pretty much reduced to making a living through self-employment, mainly in small family-run laundries and restaurants. Their forced segregation into ethnically isolated, marginal industries and urban ghettos provided yet another reason for white Americans to dislike them: the Chinese could now be also scorned for their insular ways.

Amah With Child, San Francisco Chinatown, c. 1895. **Photo by Arnold Genthe. This was not a typical Chinatown scene, since in 1890 Chinese men in the United States outnumbered Chinese women by 27 to 1. Naturally, children were few also.**

Because they were almost completely isolated from the outside, Chinese ethnic ghettos quickly fell under the control of traditional Chinese associations. These traditional organizations were formed by people from the same family, village, region, or trade, to safeguard their interests and provide aid. But in the context of American Chinatowns, a new form of association, based on the secrecy of its membership and on sworn allegiance to the organization itself, sprung up to fill the vacuum left by the absence of white authorities. Usually known as *tongs*, these secret societies quickly assumed the role of community law enforcement agencies. They organized their own "soldiers," called "Brave Tigers," for self-defense, but also to promote and enforce the interests of the wealthy members of the community. The social and political order in Chinatowns came to depend on the precarious balance of power among the most powerful tongs, kept in check by an umbrella organization known in most instances as the Chinese Consolidated Benevolent Association. When the umbrella organization was unable to resolve conflicts, the result was violence and even "tong wars."

One very peculiar feature of Chinese urban ghettos was the scarcity of women. The Chinese Labor Exclusion Act of 1882 defined Chinese women as laborers, so the Chinese laborers who were already in the country before its passage could not bring the wives and families they had left behind.

"Queen of Chinatown."
A magazine illustration promoting the commonly held view that Chinatowns were unsanitary, dangerous places teaming with houses of ill repute, where a white person could only expect to be trapped—if lured by the vices of illicit sex, gambling, or opium— to enter its shady world.

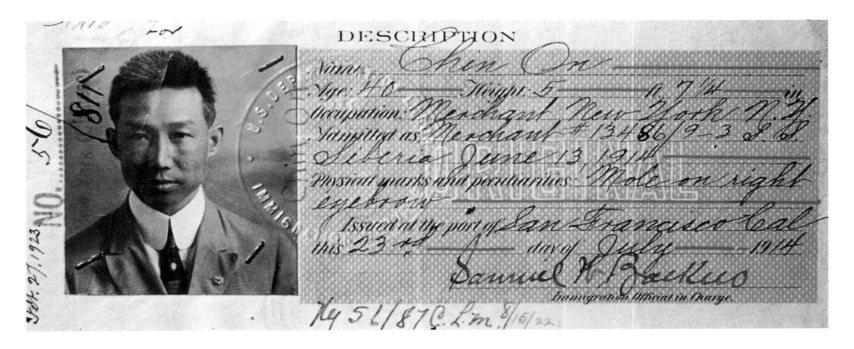

ORIGINAL

Those who were not yet married ended up as lifelong bachelors. The only Chinese men in the United States fortunate enough to have families were those with merchant status. (Merchants, teachers, and students were not banned by the Exclusion Act.) Consequently, a family with children was a rare sight in Chinese American communities until World War II.

It is this experience of forced isolation that made most Chinese in the United States develop the "sojourner mentality." It forced them to think in terms of a short-term stay: they wanted to make enough money in the shortest possible time so they could go back to China to start their families.

An identity card for merchant Chin On, issued in San Francisco July 23, 1914, with the seal of the U.S. Department of Immigration. Only merchants, students, teachers, government officials, visitors, and the Chinese who could claim U.S. citizenship were admitted to the United States after the passage of the Exclusion Act.

ALTERNATIVES

Despite considerable obstacles, many Chinese remained in the United States and found unique ways to improve their situation.

Some built families through smuggling. Others used the ploy of declaring "paper sons"—legally bringing into the country relatives or unrelated boys, who paid to be claimed as sons conceived in China, and presented appropriate papers to justify their claims. Chinese entering the country were all subjected to extensive interrogation, and those immigrants who claimed fictitious relations prepared themselves by memorizing facts about family, home life, and native village from "coaching books" that were often taken aboard ships and thrown overboard or destroyed as the ship approached American shores.

A well-to-do merchant family's wedding group portrait, Idaho City, Idaho, 1906. Only merchants were able to bring wives from China, since their immigration status was not restricted by the Chinese Exclusion Act of 1882, which targeted "laborers." According to the United States census of 1870, almost 59 percent of the miners in Idaho were Chinese. Even after the mines dried up, the Chinese who showed resourcefulness in finding untapped job opportunities remained in the area. Some of them became truck-gardeners; others worked providing food and laundering services to the communities where they settled. The most successful among them were usually the merchants.

After the San Francisco earthquake of 1906 and the ensuing fire in which all city records were lost, many Chinese were able to claim that they were U.S. citizens. As such, they were allowed to bring in their offspring, but not their Chinese-born wives. During the 1910s and 1920s, economic and political conditions in China grew worse due to continued civil strife, division, and encroachment of foreign colonial powers, so a growing number of relatives were brought to the United States to work in family-owned businesses as additional free labor, thus helping fledging Chinese businesses in the accumulation of the capital.

United States immigration officials took harsh measures to restrict illegal entries. They often conducted sweeps of Chinese establishments to catch illegal immigrants. They also held suspect all Chinese claims for legal right of admission at ports of entry until they could conduct intensive and detailed interrogations.

The Chinese addressed numerous complaints to the United States government about the harsh treatment and discourteous behavior by immigration officials. They formed civil rights organizations and raised funds to hire

Cheong Wo & Co, San Francisco Chinatown, California, c. 1900. A typical Chinese-owned grocery shop, selling produce, meat, and imported dry goods from China. Such businesses sprung up in all places with even a small concentration of Chinese—places as far flung as Holyoke, Massachusetts; Olympia, Washington; and Lake Providence, Louisiana.

(Left) **A Chinese man among ruins after the earthquake and fire, Chinatown, San Francisco, California, 1906. Photo by Arnold Genthe. One won't easily forget this haunting image of a lone figure contemplating the desolation of the earthquake. The loss of all city records in the fire, however, made it possible for many Chinese to claim U.S. citizenship, thus allowing them to bring in their offspring (although not their Chinese-born wives).**

(Following spread) **"Made in Mott Street. The rest of New York moves, but Chinatown stays." Typically negative caricatures of Chinese Americans in Chinatown.**

lawyers to better challenge the overtly hostile, restrictive legislation in courts. In a majority of instances, their court challenges were successful. In a precedent-setting ruling in 1898, in the case of "Wong Kim Ark, Native Born Citizen of the United States," the Supreme Court established that United States-born descendants of immigrants could not be denied U.S. citizenship, regardless of their ethnicity or the nationality of their ancestors.

Usually known as servile and submissive, the Chinese even held public demonstrations to protest their treatment. Fifteen thousand Chinese gathered in New York on June 15, 1901, to take part in a mass demonstration

Grandpa

"Allee same
Mellican boy"

食点包

They like sweet
potatoes baked
in a pushcart
oven

Curb
sitters

Mott Street

A Sketch

Always Suspicious

In holiday costume

It cant be base-
ball scores but
it's something
equally interest-
ing

How they
love to loaf

OTT STREET

A CLOSER LOOK:
CHILDREN IN CHINATOWN

The only Chinese men in the United States fortunate enough to have families were those with merchant status. (Merchants, teachers, and students were not banned by the Exclusion Act.) Consequently, families with children were a rare sight in Chinese American communities until World War II.

Having male offspring is very important to the Chinese since, according to Chinese culture, it is the boys who carry the family line. All little boys are indulged in Chinese families, and the ones such as these photographed by Arnold Genthe in San Francisco's Chinatown are no exception. The photograph on the right, taken in 1897, is often reproduced under the title, *The Little Aristocrats,* which is clearly how the less fortunate, sonless Chinese laborers would have seen the merchants' little boys.

(Opposite) Dressed for success. A Chinese-American businessman in traditional Chinese silk clothing, New York, 1915.

condemning the restrictive laws against them—an event which the *New York Tribune* covered on its front page. In 1905, Chinese-American merchants joined a boycott of American goods, which had started in Shanghai to protest American immigration procedures, and quickly spread to Canton, other Chinese cities, and overseas Chinese communities. The boycott was sustained for several months and forced the United States to relax some of the more objectionable regulations. But the negative attitude toward Chinese immigration remained strong in the country, and the Exclusion Law, originally set to last ten years, was repeatedly renewed and reinforced, remaining in effect until 1943.

BRANCHING OUT

While most Chinese concentrated in large urban centers on the West and East coasts, some sought their fortunes in areas that the anti-Chinese agitators and organizations had not penetrated, where the anti-Chinese sentiment was weak. Those were usually places without a strong Chinese presence in the past—Midwestern and Southern towns like Kokomo, Indiana; Little Rock, Arkansas; or New Orleans and Baton Rouge, Louisiana. They were quite successful as merchants in places as far-flung as Holyoke, Massachusetts; Olympia, Washington; and Lake Providence, Louisiana. But most found work as farm laborers and farmhands, grocers, and launderers.

In California, where the Chinese could not own land because of the 1913 Alien Land Act, they could be found cultivating vineyards and building cellars for some of the oldest wineries, such as Beringer, in the state's emerging wine region. They also provided crucial manpower in the state's first apple orchards in the Pajaro Valley near Santa Cruz, which were pioneered by Slavic immigrants from the Dalmatian coast of the Mediterranean Sea. Although by 1890 the Slavs dominated the local apple industry, some Chinese merchants succeeded in setting up their own apple-packing businesses, and made a name for themselves when they managed to take over the labor-intensive apple-drying operations in the area. They leased the large tray-loaded drying kilns from the Slav growers and became so skillful

(Opposite) "Chicago
Street Type," c. 1900.

in operating them that the kilns became known as the "China Dryers," and they dominated the Pajaro Valley apple-drying industry during the first decades of this century.

Many Chinese were also able to pool their resources and lease land, on which they grew vegetables that they sold in towns. By 1900, Santa Cruz was completely encircled by Chinese gardens, from which Chinese peddlers carried baskets of produce early each morning to sell on the streets: cabbage, lettuce, okra, yams, raspberries, gooseberries, blackberries— depending on the season—and fresh strawberries as early as February. In the Sacramento-San Joaquin Delta, where they had worked as agricultural laborers on land reclamation projects in the 1870s, they grew cash crops such as sugar beets, tomatoes, corn, beans, asparagus, and fruit (especially pears). The majority of them leased small tracts of land that required the labor of no more than ten people, and they employed other Chinese laborers to work with them. A few engaged in tenant farming on a large scale, leasing over a thousand acres. The most successful and famous were Chin Lung (also called Sing Kee), the "Potato King" of the 1910s; Thomas Foon Chew, the "Asparagus King" of the 1920s; and Lincoln Chan, the "Pear King" of the 1950s.

Also, it was a Chinese squirrel trapper, "Poison Jim," who turned wild mustard plants, growing weed-like in the Salinas Valley, into a valuable commercial crop. He contracted a few dozen fellow Chinese to cut the plants and remove the seeds, and when the entire mustard crop failed in both Europe and South Africa, he literally got $35,000 in gold for his bagged seeds.

Fishing and related food-processing industries continued to provide a livelihood for many Chinese on the West Coast. Particularly in the Monterey Bay region, where the Chinese existed with little friction with their Hispanic, English, Portuguese, and Italian neighbors, Chinese fishermen continued to catch and dry fish, shrimp, squid, abalone, and seaweed, and to process the by-products of fish canneries into fertilizer. Since most of the dried seafood was shipped overseas to be sold, the fishing industry gave rise

to a flourishing import and export business with China, a number of Chinese-owned steamship companies, and the establishment of local Chinese banks to finance the Chinese-owned operations. Chinese entrepreneurs found a niche for themselves in which they did not compete directly with white Americans: they used Chinese laborers, sold their goods and services to the Chinese, and financed themselves through Chinese savings. By 1935, however, no Chinese commercial fishermen were left in the Monterey region because of immigration restrictions, death, return of the early pioneers to China, and municipal restrictions that targeted the seafood-processing operations.

While it is clear that Chinese immigrants were able to do well in America when they could use the skills they had brought with them from China—

"China Annie," sold to a member of the Yeong Wo Company in Idaho City to work as a prostitute, escaped to Boise to marry her lover, Ah Guan. A sympathetic judge dismissed her owner's charge of grand larceny for stealing herself and granted her freedom.

particularly in agriculture, fishing, and the food-processing industries—there were some genuinely adventuresome characters among them who sought alternatives to urban ghetto existence by remaining in the once booming towns of the "Wild West." Some even became cowboys. But most showed little interest in the shootings, knifings, and gun battles, and instead opened eateries that catered to the cowmen, rustlers, lawmen, gunfighters, gamblers, and miners alike. Some of the most colorful Chinese-American characters have left their mark on western lore in faraway places like Warrens, Idaho, and Tombstone, Arizona.

Polly Bemis was born into poverty in northern China in 1853, sold for two bags of seed to bandits, shipped to America as a slave, and auctioned off to

a Chinese saloon keeper in a mining camp of Warrens, Idaho. She worked as a prostitute in the saloon until Charlie Bemis won her in a poker game and married her. She became a well-liked and respected member of the community, so much so that when she died in 1933, members of the Grangeville City Council served as her pallbearers, and a creek running through her property was named Polly Creek.

One of the most famous eateries in Tombstone, Arizona, was called the Can-can. It was co-owned by Ah Lum and Quong Gee Kee, who was, when he died in 1938, the last surviving Chinese resident of the legendary town. He counted Wyatt Earp and others of O.K. Corral fame among his clientele, and he was notoriously kind to his customers—even to wild cowboys who ransacked his restaurant in a drunken rage. He refused to have the culprits arrested, claiming they would get mad and never pay up, and he'd only lose good customers. He maintained that they would be sorry when they sobered up, and so they were: they came back a week later to pay for the damage. He never sued anybody. His philosophy was: "No go to court. When they have money they pay. In court, lawyer take money. Then

Polly Bemis at her Salmon River ranch near Warrens, Idaho. Charlie Bemis won Polly in a poker game at the Chinese saloon in a mining camp of Warrens, Idaho, where she worked as a prostitute, and married her. They settled on the banks of the Salmon River where she came to be highly regarded for her tireless contributions to the community.

Quong have no money, no friends." He died penniless, but one of the best-liked figures in Tombstone. His friends collected a sizable fund to bury him in style at Tombstone's Boothill Cemetery, and Roland Bridges, Maine state senator, delivered the eulogy at his graveside. A local old-timer, a mule skinner during Tombstone's heyday, remarked: "I guess old Quong had just about the biggest funeral ever held on Boothill. I've seen about fifty folks buried up here, and not one of them ever had any five hundred people turn out to see them get planted. It was far superior to any planting I ever watched there, even better than any Democrat's."

"China Mary" of Tombstone, Arizona. In rural areas, most Chinese women ended up with the name "China Mary," given to them out of disregard by their white neighbors. Nevertheless, each "China Mary" led a unique life. This "China Mary" was Mary Lum, whose husband, Ah Lum, co-owned one of the most famous eateries in town. Called the Can-can, their restaurant was frequented by the likes of Wyatt Earp and the O.K. Corral gang.

Ah Lum's wife in Tombstone was known as China Mary. "China Mary" was a generic name given to most Chinese women in rural areas by their white neighbors out of disdain and prejudice. Yet each China Mary led a unique life. China Mary of Sitka, Alaska, ran away from her riverboat home in China when she was nine and worked her way to Canada when she was thirteen. Widowed twice, she settled in Sitka, where she learned English and the language of the Tlingit Indians, and worked as fisher, hunter, prospector, cook, restaurant and laundry operator, dairy and fox farmer, midwife, nurse, and official matron of the federal jail. China Mary of Evanston, Wyoming, outlived three wealthy Chinese husbands and died at the age of one hundred in 1939. She, too, could speak English, and always made a point of participating in Evanston's annual Cowboy Days celebration. Even China Mary of Oakdale, California, who was adopted with her brother by the non-Chinese Moulton family and given the name Mary Moulton, was still better known as China Mary.

The grave of Mary Lum, known as "China Mary," at the Boothill Cemetery in Tombstone, Arizona. Several other Chinese residents of Tombstone chose to be buried on Boothill, rather than have their bones returned to China, as custom dictated.

STAYING IN TOUCH WITH THE OLD COUNTRY

Treatment of the ethnic Chinese in the United States seemed to be a direct reflection of the stature China enjoyed on the international stage. By the end of the nineteenth century, Americans, like all the other Western nations, viewed China and its nationals with scorn. Consequently, some Chinese in the United States, desperate to gain the respect of their white American compatriots, conceived of a deliberate strategy: helping China to become strong. This was particularly important to those Chinese who had spent decades in the United States without hope of ever becoming American

A CLOSER LOOK:
"BLACK JACK" AND
THE CHINESE

When General John "Black Jack" Pershing received orders to end his Punitive Expedition into Mexico (launched to capture "Pancho" Villa) and return to the United States in 1916, he had 527 Chinese attached to his expeditionary force. They had served him loyally; their shops, laundries, and restaurants had dotted the entire route from Columbus, Texas, to his headquarters in the Mexican desert, providing service to his ten thousand troops. Moreover, whenever the latest-issue machinery failed in the wilds of the Chihuahua mountains and the breakdown of the Quartermaster Corps left American troops stranded in enemy territory, it was the Chinese who saved them by hauling in provisions by mule, two-horse wagon, and foot. "Pancho" Villa was bent on killing them. "Black Jack" Pershing insisted on bringing them back with him to the United States. He saw it as a debt of honor. This was no mean feat—not even for a general who would soon become "General of the Armies of the United States." The 1882 Exclusion Act was in effect, and the general had to lobby Congress for five years before the "Pershing Chinese" were admitted as permanent residents (U.S. citizenship was denied), as long as the military guaranteed that they would not become a public charge. The army promptly put them to work as cooks and in other utility tasks.

This was not the only time the Chinese risked their lives for a United States cause. Forty-seven fought in the Civil War, on both sides of the conflict. Hundreds dug trenches for the allied forces in France during World War I. During World War II, some fifteen thousand were employed on "Liberty Ships" ferrying supplies from America to the besieged allies in Europe.

(Above) **Reception for General John J. Pershing at Ellington Field, Texas, by the Chinese, February 6, 1920.** *(Right)* **General Pershing and his troops.**

citizens. A politically modernized and economically developed China would be strong enough to stand up to Western nations, protect its nationals abroad, and improve their image in the eyes of white Americans. Many disenfranchised Chinese living in America saw helping China as a way to help themselves.

As it was clear that China's Manchu imperial government could not stop the decline begun with the encroachment of Western colonial powers, Chinese Americans readily supported all kinds of anti-colonial, anti-imperial, and nationalistic movements in China that promised reform or even revolution. In fact, when Sun Yat-sen, the founder of the Nationalist (Guomindang, or KMT) Party and the father of the Chinese republican revolution, first started enlisting support for his anti-Manchu ideas, he traveled to Hawaii, where he had studied at a missionary school in his teens. There, in 1894, with the help of his brother and other prominent Chinese acquaintances from the islands, he established his first political party, the Revive China Society (Xingzhong hui). The primary goal of this organization was to raise money for an anti-Manchu uprising in China. Five years later, Kang Youwei founded the Reform Party (Baohuang hui) in Vancouver, Canada, aiming to reform the crumbling Qing imperial government; later he found crucial support among the Chinese in California, Hawaii, New York, Boston, Philadelphia, Cincinnati, Ohio, and Hartford, Connecticut. In the first decade of the twentieth century, many other politicians from China toured the United States with the same purpose of enlisting material support for their causes back home. Many political organizations and parties established Chinese-language newspapers in the United States, and the most die-hard members of the Reform Party, which by then had switched to a revolutionary agenda, financed or joined the cadet school in Los Angeles in 1903 to train for antigovernment military engagement in China.

These political activities were critical for the life of the Chinese-American community. They gave Chinese Americans, who were largely excluded from participation in American economic, social, and political life, a sense of purpose and commitment. The effects were particularly positive when

it came to the lives of Chinese-American youth. They took great pride in the establishment of the Chinese Republic in 1911, which was modeled on Western democracies and was expected to propel China into the modern world.

In the following decades China was ravaged by a civil war, and its regions fell under the control of various warlords. During this period, no single party or movement could claim the absolute loyalty of the overseas Chinese communities in the United States, which were generally ready to lend their support to any group that appeared to be fighting for China. For a time after 1923, when the newly reorganized Nationalist Party (KMT or Guomindang) began to coordinate the patriotic movements on a mass

Legal photograph of Dr. Sun Yat-sen, the father of the Chinese republican revolution, contained in his investigative case file at the San Francisco District Office of the Immigration and Naturalization Service. The photograph was taken on March 28, 1910, merely a year before his movement overthrew the Manchu imperial dynasty and he became the first President of the Republic of China.

level, Chinese Americans from all walks of life and political factions joined the cause. But nothing united them more than the KMT call for an organized response to Japan's intrusion in China's Shandong Province in 1928, which resulted in the formation of the Chinese Citizens' Patriotic League of New York and various other anti-Japanese groups throughout the country. At this time, over one hundred Chinese Americans returned to China to teach in universities and colleges such as Lingnan University, St. John's Shanghai University, Peking Union Medical College, and Yanjing University. Then, when a full-scale war broke out between China and Japan in 1937 after Japan occupied a good chunk of China, ninety-one Chinese American organizations sent representatives to an emergency meeting in San Francisco and founded the China War Relief Association of America. The association raised funds for the financially troubled Nationalist government in China, organized demonstrations and anti-Japanese parades, encouraged a boycott of Japanese merchandise, and picketed shipyards in Los Angeles; Everett, Washington; and Astoria, Oregon, in an attempt to stop Japanese ships from carrying out of American harbors scrap iron and other raw materials to be used in Japan's war effort in China. The effort of Chinese Americans to win the support of the American public for the anti-Japanese cause before Japan attacked Pearl Harbor is usually known as "People's Diplomacy." On the more militant side, thirty-three young Chinese-American pilots from Portland, Oregon, joined the Nationalist air force to fight Japan's military aggression in China directly.

Chinese Revolutionary Headquarters and Flag, Chinatown, New York City. Chinese Americans actively supported all kinds
of anti-colonial, anti-imperial, and nationalistic movements in China that promised to reform the ineffective Manchu imperial government,
or even revolution. To many, America's own anti-colonial, anti-imperial revolution served as inspiration. From 1880 to 1910,
Chinese politicians toured the United States, and many political parties set up headquarters in Chinese-American communities
in California, Hawaii, New York, Connecticut, Massachusetts, Pennsylvania, and Ohio.

A CLOSER LOOK:
ANGEL ISLAND

Angel Island Immigration Station served as a point of entry for the majority of Chinese immigrants to America between 1910 and 1940—some 175,000 people in all. It was built in 1910, modeled after New York's Ellis Island, to replace a two-story shed at the Pacific Mail Steamship Company wharf, which had until then served to detain Chinese immigrants until they passed medical examinations and until immigration inspectors could establish the validity of their application claims. Although modern in amenities and style, it reflected the climate set by the Exclusion Act of 1882 and its subsequent revisions that further tightened the provisions for admitting Chinese into the United States and was designed to exclude rather than to admit. Its very location in the San Francisco Bay, not far from the infamous Alcatraz prison, was chosen to make it escape-proof.

The immigrants were kept at the station, sometimes for months, in crowded dormitories behind locked doors, while being subjected to rigorous interrogations. Since most needed interpreters, a different one was used for each interrogation session to prevent collusion. The applicants who were not approved were deported back to China; those who appealed to the courts remained on Angel Island for as long as two years to await reverse decision. Some could not bear the disappointment and committed suicide. Others committed their frustrations to the detention center's walls by carving Chinese-character poems into the wood. This unique cultural heritage has been preserved, within the Angel Island State Park, thanks to the effort of the local Asian-American community.

(Above) **Angel Island Immigration Station, California, c. 1924.** *(Right)* **Quarantine inspection of passengers on a trans-Pacific liner docked at Angel Island, California, February 1924.**

PARTIAL ACCEPTANCE

After the bombing of Pearl Harbor, the United States entered World War II on the same side as China. The two countries became allies in the Pacific theater of war. This had enormous consequences for the Chinese in America. No longer despised, Chinese people were suddenly portrayed in American media as heroic fighters against fascism. *Time* magazine voted Chiang Kai-shek, the Nationalist leader who had succeeded Sun Yat-sen, as its "Man of the Year" in 1941. His wife, Madame Chiang Kai-shek, was invited to visit the United States in 1943 by President Franklin D. Roosevelt, who insisted that China be treated as a major power. Since she had been educated in America and spoke fluent English, Madame Chiang proved to be an exceptional ambassador, and her visit did much to improve the situation of the Chinese Americans. Her impassioned speech to a joint session of Congress on February 18 aroused American sympathy for the plight of China, and presented a new image of the Chinese people to the American public. And, as American attitudes toward China improved, so did the treatment of Chinese in the United States. Chinese Americans were now portrayed in the mainstream newspapers like *The New York Times*, *The San Francisco Examiner*, and *The Los Angeles Times*, as intelligent, tolerant, modern, proud, and Christian.

One reflection of the changing attitudes in America was the portrayal of the Chinese in Hollywood movies. During the period of anti-Chinese

(Opposite) **"American Way." 1942. American Boy Scouts are fiercely proud of their Americanism and what it means: Freedom and Equality For All. The smiling face of the young Chinese-American member of Troop 150 radiates the feeling that during World War II that ideal for the first time came within reach of Chinese immigrants in America.**

prejudice, the images of Chinese on American screens were decidedly unfavorable. Chinese were usually depicted as debased and laughable *(Fun in a Chinese Laundry*, 1894), as half-witted, inept fools providing comic relief (*Chinese Rubbernecks,* 1903), as unscrupulous and cowardly villains (*The Yellow Menace,* 1916), or gangsters (*Chinatown Nights,* 1930, and *The Hatchet Man,* 1932). They were played by white actors who wore Chinese shirts and baggy pants, and sported hairpieces in the style of Qing dynasty Manchu pigtails. Often cast in smoky interiors, where long-nailed figures holding daggers lurked in the shadows, the projected image of the Chinese-American world was one of white slavery, kidnapping, opium smoking, and heathen rites—designed to evoke fear of a threat to Western civilization. No one personified it better than Dr. Fu Manchu, evil incarnate. Alternately played by Warner Oland and Boris Karloff between 1926 and 1932 and revisited by Peter Sellers in 1980, the diabolical madman with his clawlike outstretched hands, feline eyes, and characteristic goatee, remains to this day an icon of the American cultural imagination. But, perhaps indicative of the

Anna May Wong, the first Asian star in American cinema, at home in Hollywood, California, c. 1934. When other Chinese-American actors were relegated to supporting roles as cooks, servants, laundrymen, or gangsters, she was cast as the "vamp" in many 1920s silent films. She could not, however, escape the racial stereotyping in Hollywood in the 1920s and 1930s.

"Make peace with your father ~~~"

1336·131

changing times, the persona of a wise, witty and mild-mannered "master sleuth," the enigmatic Chinese-American detective, Charlie Chan, also emerged in 1926, and went on to captivate American audiences for two and a half decades through forty-eight feature films, numerous books, magazines, comic-strips, theater, and radio and television shows. The creation of the sympathetic detective reflected Hollywood's attempt to refashion the American image of the Chinese during the years of diplomatic goodwill and the wartime alliance between the United States and China against expansionist Japan. Many movies made at that time, such as *The Good Earth*, or *The Inn of Sixth Happiness*, depict China in a similarly favorable light.

When it comes to Chinese Americans however, one of the most far-reaching consequences of the wartime alliance between the two nations and the resulting new attitudes toward things Chinese was the repeal of the Chinese Exclusion Act in 1943. Immediately after Madame Chiang's visit

In the 1931 movie, *Daughter of the Dragon*, Anna May Wong played the murderous daughter of the evil Dr. Fu Manchu (played by Warner Oland) shown in the still above.

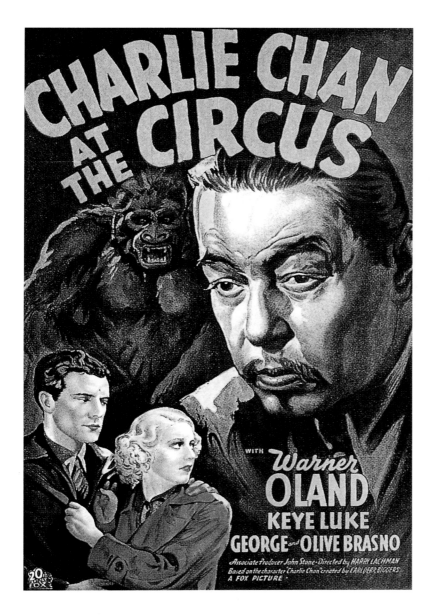

The brilliant, enigmatic detective Charlie Chan emerged in 1926 as a new type of Chinese-American on the Hollywood screen. He proved so popular that over the next two and a half decades Hollywood released forty-eight Charlie Chan movies in all, and spawned a whole Charlie Chan comic-strip, radio-show, theater, book and magazine industry. As one of the more enduring Hollywood creations of the "talkie" era, many of the films are still played on classic American film channels today. The popular fictional character of Charlie Chan was always played by a white actor, however, "face-painted" to look Chinese, who would affect a Chinese accent and mannerisms entertaining to white audiences. *Charlie Chan's Chance (opposite), Charlie Chan at the Circus (above left),* and *Charlie Chan on Broadway (above right),* all starred Warner Oland in the title role.

(Above) Movie still from
*Charlie Chan in
Honolulu*, 1938, starring
Sen Yung and Sidney
Toler. (Left) *Charlie Chan
at the Race Track*, 1936,
with Warner Oland in
the Charlie Chan role.

to Capitol Hill in February 1943, the Committee on Immigration and Naturalization began hearings on various bills designed to repeal the Chinese exclusion laws and to place the Chinese on a quota basis. President Roosevelt himself sent a message to the House of Representatives supporting the House Resolution 3070, saying:

> *We must be big enough to acknowledge our mistakes of the past and to correct them. By the repeal of the Chinese exclusion laws, we can correct a historic mistake and silence the distorted Japanese propaganda. The enactment of legislation now pending before Congress would put Chinese immigrants on a parity with those from other countries . . . While it would give the Chinese a preferred status over a certain Oriental people, their contribution to the cause of decency and freedom entitled them to such preference.*

Since the so-called Magnuson bill was introduced under the extraordinary circumstances of wartime, it was almost certainly destined to pass. It enjoyed an overwhelming majority of support. The House passed it only ten days after President Roosevelt sent his message; the Senate approved it a month later. On December 17, 1943, President Roosevelt signed it into law, reversing a policy of sixty years, which had been left in effect by thirty Congresses.

The new bill allowed a yearly quota of 105 Chinese immigrants into the United States, regardless of their place of birth. Although this quota was much lower than that set for European immigrants, and although other discriminatory laws remained in effect (Chinese schoolchildren were segregated throughout the country; Chinese workers were not allowed to hold public employment; miscegenation laws still existed in at least eighteen states), it still brought about a major change in the life of Chinese Americans. When the bill went into effect, more than half of all Chinese in America—some forty thousand—were foreign born. As a result of the new legislation they became eligible for U.S. citizenship. The bill also signaled a new era in Sino-American relations. After 1944, an increasing number of non-quota Chinese immigrants, such as scholars, were allowed into the

The Good Earth, starring Paul Muni and Louise Rainer, was released in 1937 as one of the first movies made in Hollywood that attempted to portray China and its people with sympathy. It was based on the novel of the same title by Pearl Buck, which won a Pulitzer Prize for fiction in 1932. Although Hollywood tried to portray the Chinese in a more positive light, now that the two countries were allied against Japan, all the Chinese characters in the movie were still played by white actors.

country: while before only ten came on the average each year, now 137 arrived annually to teach in the United States. But, most importantly, the repeal of the Chinese Exclusion Act had a morale-boosting effect on the many Chinese who were drafted or enlisted in the United States armed services—approximately twelve thousand in all—and for those who worked on the assembly lines supporting the war effort.

Because of the wartime manpower shortage, Chinese Americans were given job opportunities in industries that had been previously closed to them.

Wong Ruth Mae Moy, working on an aircraft engine part, c. 1943. During World War II, due to severe manpower shortages, many Chinese were recruited to work in industries related to national defense.

President Franklin D. Roosevelt issued an executive order calling for an end to racial discrimination, with an explanation that it is "only through the unity of all people that we can successfully win the war, regardless of race, color, and creed." A massive mobilization was needed in all industries related to national defense, and many Chinese, along with members of other minority groups, were suddenly released from their low-paying "ghetto" service jobs to find employment in mainstream industries. Chinese joined the shipyard workforce in the San Francisco Bay area, the Seattle-Tacoma area, in Delaware, and in Mississippi. Many found work in airplane factories on Long Island and in Texas, in arsenal plants in New Jersey, and in war-materials manufacturing in Alaska. Most were still shunted off to menial jobs, but an increasing number were also able to secure technical, engineering and scientific positions which paid good wages. For the first time even Chinese women entered the American workforce, as they shared in the national emergency war-production effort. Without a doubt, the war finally gave Chinese Americans an opportunity for economic integration and acceptance into American society.

Chinese-American community leaders urged young Chinese to prove themselves as loyal Americans by enlisting in the United States armed

"Yours for Victory." Young Chinese-American woman working on airplane parts in a U.S. Defense plant during World War II.

(Opposite) **Leah Hing worked as an instrument mechanic at a Portland air base during World War II. She knew a thing or two about flying engines: after earning a pilot's license in 1934 she bought and flew her own plane.**

forces. Many heeded the call. In the New York metropolitan area alone, four thousand young men enlisted at the very beginning of the war to the cheers of their community. In Butte, Montana, each one of the eleven Chinese residents of draft age enlisted voluntarily. Over 20 percent of the 59,803 adult Chinese males in the United States (including citizens, residents, and students) enlisted or were drafted by the U.S. Army. A smaller number served in the Air Force, and five hundred were recruited as apprentice seamen by the U.S. Navy.

In addition, some fifteen thousand Chinese nationals were employed on "Liberty Ships"—the United States and British ships that carried supplies from American shores to the war-besieged nations of Great Britain and the Soviet Union. So many of these ships had been sunk by the early 1940s by German U-boats patrolling the North Atlantic that the casualties suffered by the merchant marine on the supply convoys surpassed even U.S. Navy losses sustained in the first year of active American engagement in the war. Chinese seamen were hired in Hong Kong for duty on these highly perilous missions. They suffered staggering casualties, and even though, as aliens, they were not allowed to take shore leave in the United States during the war, their service was deemed meritorious enough to grant those who survived the right to become U.S. citizens after the war.

Perhaps the most celebrated case among the survivors is that of Poon Lim, a native of Hainan Island in southern China, who worked as the second steward on the SS *Benlomond* when it was torpedoed by a German submarine and sank off the coast of Brazil on November 23, 1942. He was picked up by fishermen 133 days later at the mouth of the Amazon River. Although he was thirty pounds underweight, naked, and sunburned, he was able to walk off his raft onto the fishermen's boat, and later onto shore unassisted. His ordeal as a sole shipwreck survivor at sea remains unmatched to this day.

Poon Lim was honored with the United States Merchant Marine Combat Bar with One Star by special order of the War Shipping Administration, and invested with the British Empire Medal by King George VI. Yet despite

these honors, being Chinese, he was prohibited from immigrating to the United States by the 1882 Exclusion Act. In an interview after he received the British Empire Medal, Poon Lim stated that, "The sea does not know the difference between the yellow man and the white man," and said he hoped "that this fact will lead to the betterment of the conditions of my

Many young men enlisted voluntarily during World War II, at the urging of Chinese-American community leaders, to prove their patriotism. (*Above*) Members of the Holy Redeemer Chinese Catholic Church in Philadelphia honor their community members who were serving the United States in 1944. (*Left*) A Navy Recruiting Station at the headquarters of the Chinese Consolidated Benevolent Association in Los Angeles, California. (*Opposite*) A Chinese resident of New York City screams for joy, having learned that Japan had capitulated, 1945. The Chinese-language newspaper in his hand, *The China Tribune,* carries the news on its front page.

Residents of New York's Chinatown anxiously follow events in the China war theatre during World War II reading Chinese-language reports posted daily on community bulletin boards.

fellow seamen and stewards, not only during the war but after the war." Although the struggle for legal equality would still be an uphill battle for his fellow Chinese, the wartime experience provided inroads into the mainstream job market. Many Chinese, including women, were able to keep the jobs they had obtained during the war, and many others grew confident enough to seek work outside Chinatowns. In some cases their efforts to gain economic equality through job opportunities were helped by progressive labor unions—most notably by the National Maritime Union, the largest maritime union in the United States, whose constitution allowed for "no discrimination against any union member because of his race, color, political affiliation, creed, religion, or national origin," and with whose support more Chinese seamen were hired during the postwar years.

The National Maritime Union also called for legislation that would give the right of naturalization to all foreign seamen who had worked on United States vessels for more than three years during the war. The U.S. Congress rejected this call, but it did pass other legislation that influenced Chinese-American community life in the most profound way. Under the War Brides Act of 1945 and the Act of August 9, 1946, alien wives of World War II veterans and U.S. citizens were permitted to come to the United States as non-quota immigrants. This legislation brought some six thousand Chinese women into the country as brides of Chinese-American servicemen. Between 1944 and 1953, women made up 82 percent of all Chinese immigrants to America. For the first time, the number of Chinese women and families in the United States noticeably increased. The male-female ratio among Chinese Americans dramatically decreased: from 27 to 1 in 1890, to 1.89 to 1 in 1950 (and further, to 1.3 to 1 in 1960). The arrival of women was followed by an explosion in the birthrate of Chinese Americans. By 1950, 54 percent of Chinese Americans were American-born.

Another result of the new climate of acceptance immediately following World War II was that Chinese Americans became active in American politics. The Chinese American Voters League was formed to encourage political participation through voting. In the late 1940s, the League mobilized Chinese-American voters to vote for more liberal candidates who advocated an end to American intervention in China's civil war. During the 1948 presidential election, for instance, the Chinese were mobilized to vote for Henry Wallace, who ran as a third-party candidate on the Progressive

American-born Chinese actress Barbara Jane Wong and movie star Walter Pidgeon read for the War Production Board radio program "Wool" in 1942.

Members of the Chinese Christian Church and Center in Philadelphia entertain servicemen on leave in 1945.

Party ticket, since he was the only candidate to come out against United States intervention in China's domestic affairs.

Unfortunately, the Cold War era brough a cruel "reversal of fortunes" for many Chinese Americans. The progress they made in the 1930s and 1940s in making inroads into American society was stunted because of the United States involvement with China's affairs. In 1949, communists defeated nationalists on China's mainland and established the People's Republic of China, and American attitudes soured when it came to China and the Chinese. When, in 1951, the outbreak of the Korean War brought American troops in direct confrontation with the commmunist Chinese army, the latent animosity turned to open belligerence, and Chinese Americans were once again subjected to hostility on the domestic front. Many found themselves accused of being sympathetic to China's communist regime and suspected of disloyalty to the United States.

Many white Americans also came under investigation by the United States House of Representatives Committee on Un-American Activities, which conducted widely publicized "witch-hunts" against "radical agitators," "Communist sympathizers," and "fellow travelers" during the 1940s and 1950s. Nationalist leader Chiang Kai-shek's supporters took advantage of the repressive climate to set up a conservative network, known as the "China Lobby," which included congressmen, military officials, business-men, scholars, and journalists. With the help of the House Un-American Activities Committee, "China Lobby" effectively persecuted all those criti-cal of the nationalist regime, including many of America's best-known China specialists, such as Edgar Snow, Pearl Buck, and Theodore White, who all ended up on Senator McCarthy's infamous blacklist. Anybody who dared voice an opinion critical of the Nationalist government on Taiwan or Chiang Kai-shek was immediately labeled as "red."

Barbara Wong of Canton, China, was the first Chinese war-bride to be married in the United States, on January 25, 1947, in San Francisco, California, under provisions of the War Brides Act of 1945. Alien wives of World War II veterans were permitted to come to the United States as non-quota immigrants.

The hardest hit by the pervasive red-baiting—due to their implied association with their ancestral land, "Red China"—were the Americans of Chinese descent. Under the 1950 Internal Security Act, virtually all Chinese in the United States were considered suspect, and the State and Justice departments imposed unusually stringent requirements on all Chinese entering the country. Based on the 1955 Drumright Report, which charged massive falsification of documents by Chinese immigrants from Hong Kong, virtually all Chinese immigrants were assumed guilty until proved innocent. Between 1956 and 1965, the Immigration and Naturalization Service ran a "Confession Program," allowing its officers to prosecute all those among the illegal entrants who came forward to be registered whose political views they found questionable. Needless to say, coming just over a decade after the repeal of the Chinese Exclusion Act, the program caused widespread fear in Chinese-American communities.

The greatest beneficiaries of the renewed alienation of Chinese Americans from the American society were the traditional Chinese associations. Their influence had declined during the 1940s, as a growing number of Chinese Americans found jobs in the mainstream, joining professional unions and various independent organizations. Now, riding the wave of anti-Communism and joining hands with the Nationalist Government of Taiwan, they carried out their own red-baiting campaign to bring the Chinese community in the United States to submission. The umbrella organization of traditional associations, the Chinese Consolidated Benevolent Association (CCBA), granted one of the seven permanent positions on its executive board to Taiwan's Nationalist Party; its prominent leaders were appointed to the Taiwan National Assembly in return. Its members received exclusive trade privileges with Taiwan for their "patriotism"; the members of progressive labor and youth associations were harassed and persecuted. Under the joint assault by American conservative institutions and traditional Chinese associations, all progressive and dissenting voices in the community were silenced.

To Be an American, Off and On. An American-born girl, Lillian Ying Lu, lost her U.S. citizenship in 1920 when she married an internationally known Chinese scholar, Dr. Kiang Kanghu. She did not leave it at that. Eleven years later, in 1931, her citizenship was restored by an act of Congress. It was the first such case in U.S. history. In the photograph, she is showing the Supreme Court papers restoring her citizenship to Mrs. B.S. Matthews, chairman of the Lawyers Council of the Women's Party, while her daughter, Phoenix, watches.

THE NEW CHINESE ELITE IN AMERICA

The Communist victory in China and the cooling of relations between the United States and the People's Republic resulted in repression for many Americans of Chinese ancestry. But these events also brought about a new development in the history of Chinese immigration to America. Early Chinese immigrants were largely uneducated working-class people, with a sprinkling of merchants and entrepreneurs among them. Those Chinese who came to the United States on student visas usually returned home upon the completion of their studies. After 1949, however, some four thousand of the best-educated Chinese scholars who were attending elite institutions in the United States decided to stay in the U.S. Many other members of the economic and political elite of pre-communist China, fleeing Communist rule, found refuge in the United States as well. In sharp contrast to the earlier Chinese immigrants who were confined to urban ghettos, the members of this new group were "the cream of the crop" in China and elsewhere. They took up residence in exclusive neighborhoods corresponding to their means, and they continued to prosper in this country. Their immigrant experience was clearly very different from that of their less fortunate countrymen, and their presence in America has contributed to their new homeland in more readily recognizable and acknowledged ways. Among them one finds two winners of the Nobel Prize in Physics, T.D. Lee and C.N. Yang in 1957, "for their penetrating investigation of the so-called parity laws which has led to important discoveries regarding the elementary particles"; the computer engineer An Wang (founder of Wang Laboratories, at Lowell, Massachusetts, in 1954, who did pioneering work on magnetic core memory, the basis for all modern computer technology, and who was one of the first makers of small business calculators); the Wall Street financier of the Manhattan Fund and president of the American Can Company, Jerry Tsai; and perhaps the best-known of them all, the architect I.M. Pei (who designed Government Center in Boston, Place Ville Marie in Montreal, and the glass pyramid entrance to the Louvre Museum in Paris).

"Old China Lives on West Coast." A meeting of the Board of Chairmen of the Chinese Six Companies Benevolent Association in San Francisco's Chinatown, 1946. As the umbrella organization of traditional, conservative Chinese associations, the Benevolent Association wrested power from the more progressive organizations in the overseas Chinese communities during the Cold War. After 1949, it virtually became the voice for the Nationalist Government of Taiwan.

THE NEW ERA

Although the Chinese were one of the earliest immigrant groups to arrive in the United States of America (they arrived at the same time as the Irish, and much earlier than Italians and other Southern and Eastern Europeans), it wasn't until the civil rights movement of the 1950s and 1960s and the New Immigration Act of 1965 that the typical American experience was open to the immigrant Chinese, and that they, too, were officially allowed to reach for that elusive American dream. In 1965 the United States Congress passed a new immigration act, which reversed the racially and ethnically discrimiatory provisions of the National Origins Act of 1924, establishing a uniform annual quota of twenty thousand immigrants for every country outside of the Western Hemisphere, regardless of race or nationality.

The 1965 immigration act reflected the new spirit of equality and represented an enlightened vision, coming right on the heels of the 1964 Civil Rights Act, which outlawed racial discrimination in public accommodations and by employers, unions, and registrars of voting. The new criteria for admission to the United States became almost exclusively employment-based preferences, professional skills, and the principle of uniting family members of American citizens.

(Opposite) **A Chinese family arrives in San Francisco, California, 1956. Early Chinese immigrants were primarily poor farmers from southern coastal China. After World War II, due to the civil war in China, many scholars who were pursuing education in the United States remained in the country, and many more highly educated professionals found their way to America after 1949 to escape Chinese communist rule. Unlike their working-class countrymen who had been squeezed into ghettos, these members of the economic and political elite of pre-communist China settled in exclusive neighborhoods. They put a new face on Chinese-American identity, and their immigrant experience was very different from that of the earlier arrivals.**

The new law profoundly affected the size and composition of Chinese-American communities. For the first time the Chinese were able to legally immigrate to the United States in large numbers. The number of Chinese in the United States quickly increased from 236,084 in 1960 to 1,079,400 in 1985, and is estimated to top 2 million by the year 2000—an increase of over 100 percent every ten years since the passage of the 1965 law. The Chinese are the largest Asian group in the United States today.

Moreover, the majority of Chinese in this country at the moment are non-American born (60 percent at present). Nobody can accuse them of being sojourners any more. They are most definitely family oriented, and the gender gap that existed in the ratio of men to women for over a century was completely eliminated by 1970.

Preserving Traditional Chinese Culture in America: An American boy of Chinese descent practices Chinese calligraphy, 1952. Amidst increasing opportunities to assimilate, Chinese political organizations, schools, community and church groups strive to preserve what could soon be lost.

A child is watching the filming of the movie *On the Town*, in Chinatown, New York City, 1949. The exuberant musical, filmed on various locations across New York City reflects the tenor of the new era across the country: the war is over, and the country is growing ever more prosperous; in Chinatown, things are changing too. The Exclusion Act was finally repealed in 1943, restoring a measure of dignity to Chinese Americans. With it came new immigration—women primarily—and children, changing the face of the community.

The 3,000-plus-member Wong family reunion, Chinatown, San Francisco, 1954. Women begin to figure prominently in family and community portraits after World War II. Between 1944 and 1953, women made up 82 percent of all Chinese immigrants to America.

Also, the regional origins of the Chinese now in the United States have extended well beyond the original Cantonese with a sprinkling of Fujianese immigrants. They now come from all parts of China, particularly since the 1979 normalization of diplomatic relations between the People's Republic of China and the United States. Moreover, many Chinese these days arrive in the United States by way of secondary migrations from other parts of the world, particularly from South America and Southeast Asia. The largest secondary migrations have been from Vietnam, Malaysia, Indonesia, Thailand, and Burma, but many Chinese have also found their way to North America from places like Brazil, Peru, and Trinidad, and even less likely places such as Zimbabwe, Mauritius, and South Africa.

THE CIVIL RIGHTS MOVEMENT

Chinese Americans benefited greatly from the struggle by African-Americans to gain full citizenship rights and achieve racial equality. In the 1960s Chinese Americans began to see themselves as a part of a larger group of disadvantaged racial minorities with a common goal of fighting for social inclusion and full political recognition. With slogans like "Minorities unite! Fight for democratic rights!" and "No exclusion. Equal opportunity," Chinese activists joined the ranks of the blacks and the Latinos in the fight for economic justice, which by 1965 managed to eliminate, at least legally, housing segregation and job discrimination.

The Low family poses for a Christmas portrait, Philadelphia. The arrival of women after World War II was followed by an explosion of birthrates. By 1950, 54 percent of Chinese Americans were American-born.

Chinatown, New York, in the 1960s was controlled by the anti-communist, pro-Taiwan KMT Nationalist government community leaders. On the occasion of the arrival in New York of the delegation of the People's Republic of China to the United Nations, a banner accuses Chinese Communists of murdering 60 million people.

(Above) "For Economic Justice, Now!" A rally on the corner of Mott and Bayard Streets, Chinatown, New York, 1992. A new generation of Chinese Americans, raised in the post-war U.S., embraced the Civil Rights Movement.

(Opposite) "Minorities Unite! Fight For Democratic Rights!" Residents gather for the first democratic rights demonstration ever in New York's Chinatown, and march on City Hall, New York City, May 1975. By identifying themselves with other minorities, Chinese Americans, young and old, became participants in a larger American political movement. Photos © Corky Lee.

As it did for other racial minorities, the civil rights movement gave many Chinese a new sense of ethnic pride, while also forcing them to realize that they needed to build a new consciousness as Asian Americans—a sense of a larger collective entity, in order to combat racism against Asians as a whole. And although this Asian American form of group identity was reactive in nature, it presented the Chinese with a new strategy to fight for inclusion and equality, which led them to a number of different fronts.

By the mid-1960s a new generation of American-born Chinese was reaching adulthood. Having grown up in the more relaxed and family-oriented climate of the post-exclusion era, not in urban ghettos but in mainstream communities where the better job opportunities of the postwar era had beckoned their parents, this generation embraced the civil rights movement and through it became participants in the larger American political scene of the time. As opposition to the United States involvement in the Vietnam War grew in the late 1960s, enveloping college campuses throughout the United States, the anti-war movement enkindled unprecedented activism among young Chinese Americans entering universities. Their experience of growing up Asian in America led them to see the war differently from their white fellow-protesters; namely, as essentially a racist

International Women's Day Parade, New York City, mid-1970s. Chinese-American feminists joined with other Asian-American women to form their own contingent, to demonstrate that their concerns had been essentially overlooked by white feminists. Photo © Corky Lee.

war directed against all Asians. This view in turn shaped their understanding of two pivotal experiences of Asians in the United States; the long-lasting Chinese Exclusion, and the government-ordered internment of the United States citizens of Japanese descent during World War II.

The most radical members of the postwar generation saw themselves, and particularly the least fortunate members of the Chinese-American community still stuck in Chinatowns, as "Third World people" in the United States, equally oppressed as all other "colored" minorities in this country. Borrowing the slogan "Serve the people" from the Great Proletarian Cultural Revolution in China which inspired them, they called for the classification of Chinese communities as poverty areas in need of dramatic federal assistance, and took to the streets to demand more services for senior citizens, better child care, and decent housing. They also pressed for an end to job discrimination and for equal labor protection, for the right of Chinese Americans to join trade unions and share in the benefits of union-protected jobs in the construction industry and civil service. And, since they knew that the desirable jobs in competitive industries required education, they also rallied for the improvement of ghetto schools and demanded community control of local school boards.

"Fight to Win!" Chinatown, New York, 1976. Senior citizens, turned community activists, demand equal job opportunities for Chinese construction workers in New York City. Starting in the 1970s, Chinatown residents often protested in favor of labor protection and improved social services. Photo © Corky Lee.

Many new Chinese immigrants, particularly the untrained and uneducated women who came to the United States after 1965, benefited from the federally funded programs established in the wake of the civil rights movement, which helped them learn the language and acquire job skills. But those Chinese Americans who were born in this country and grew up without similar benefits saw themselves as historically bypassed and felt that they should be allowed to enter universities under the then widely toted "open admissions" system, which granted minorities a chance to attend public institutions of higher education in spite of, or even precisely because of considerable disadvantages in their previous education. In order to insure equal opportunities across the board, Chinese-American activists joined forces with other minority activists in demanding admission quotas for the most prestigious educational institutions in the country.

Responding to vigorous student agitation, most universities instituted changes in their college admissions and curricula, establishing "ethnic studies" programs in an attempt to set the issues affecting minorities in a more sensitive and appropriate theoretical framework.

Another offshoot of the civil rights movement that affected Chinese Americans was the growth of the feminist movement. But Chinese feminists felt that the agenda of white feminists largely bypassed the issues that affected the lives of Chinese-American

**"Stop Asian Bashing!"
Chinese Americans
protest angrily in front
of the *National Review*
offices on Lexington
Avenue, New York City,
1997. The conservative
biweekly journal of
political opinion had
labeled the Democratic
Party fundraising
scandal of 1997
"Asiagate," and in the
fallout from the
article, many Chinese
Americans found
themselves under
suspicion for fronting
for Chinese govern-
ment conspiracies by
implication. Photo
© Corky Lee.**

women, whom they defined as the victims of triple oppression: as women, as members of a minority group, and as victims of traditional Chinese values imposed on them by Chinese-American men in their homes and communities. As a result, Chinese-American women joined other women of Asian descent in forming an Asian-American feminist movement.

In the shadow of their louder and more confrontational fellow activists, some young Chinese Americans adopted a more moderate approach in combating the vestiges of inequity and poverty that defined the Chinese-American experience. They sought ways to improve the life of Chinese Americans through community projects and social reform. The projects with the broadest impact were geared toward servicing the needs of the new working-class immigrants and the aging citizens who had never left their Chinatowns. A big step in reaching the latter was the introduction of bilingual social welfare services, particularly in the realm of healthcare and other services affecting senior citizens in urban Chinese communities.

Another milestone was the introduction of bilingual education for the children of Chinese-speaking immigrants.

The entire national system of bilingual education was in fact set in motion with a landmark decision of the United States Supreme Court in a class-action suit brought by non-English-speaking Chinese students against officials responsible for the operation of the San Francisco Unified School District for violation of the Civil Rights Act of 1964. After brief arguments, the Supreme Court justices agreed with the basic charge of the lawsuit, which had been based on the failure of the San Francisco school system to provide adequate English language instruction to Chinese-speaking students, and upheld the decision in Lau *vs.* Nichols, 414 U.S. 563, on January 21, 1974. In the opinion of the Court:

> *This class suit brought by non-English-speaking Chinese students against officials responsible for the operation of the San Francisco Unified School District seeks relief against the unequal educational opportunities, which are alleged to violate, inter alia, the Fourteenth Amendment. No specific remedy is urged upon us. Teaching English to the students of Chinese ancestry who do not speak the language is one choice. Giving instructions to this group in Chinese is another. There may be others. Petitioners ask only that the Board of Education be directed to apply its expertise to the problem and rectify the situation.*

Despite significant cultural and historical differences between various ethnic groups from Asia, they were for practical reasons forced to work together and forge alliances—if for no other reason than because other Americans tended to lump them together. This was painfully demonstrated in 1982 with the murder of Vincent Chin, a young fifth-generation Chinese American, who was beaten to death in Detroit by two unemployed white autoworkers who had mistaken him for a Japanese. Although he was a draftsman and studied architecture, the two workers, resentful of the growing popularity of Japanese cars, saw him as somebody who stole their jobs, much as the lynch mobs did exactly a hundred years earlier—the year of the Chinese Exclusion Act—when they stormed through San Francisco screaming, "Kill the foreigners to save our jobs! Chinese must go!"

The murder of Vincent Chin brought Asian Americans together, because they realized that what had happened to him could just as easily happen to them. Some have even characterized his death as a historical unifying moment for Asian Americans.

PARTICIPATION IN ELECTORAL POLITICS

Asian-American participation in the political life of the United States has been a slow but steady process. For one thing, mainstream political parties have traditionally lacked interest in mobilizing Chinese-American voters due to their small numbers and relative inconsequence to the larger American political process.

Demographic distribution of Chinese-American voters has also been a problem. Educated Chinese-American professionals who vote, tend to live in scattered suburban areas and are difficult to organize into voting blocs. The Chinese Americans who live in concentrated urban ethnic communities tend to be new immigrants. They are generally poorly informed about the American political system and the Western tradition of democratic politics. In order to become full participants in the system, they need political education. But most of them are not yet U.S. citizens, and those who are, are often not registered to vote. It is only in the 1990s that local politicians have begun to court Chinese-American votes. Polls show that when Chinese Americans do vote, their vote is split almost evenly between the Democrat and Republican parties. With the exception of a few neighborhoods, Chinese Americans are thus scarcely in the position to exert political influence through their votes.

The American political process does, however, allow for a different type of political influence, namely, through financial contributions. In this area, Chinese Americans are among the most active minority groups. This does not necessarily mean that the contributors aim at benefiting their ethnic community as a whole. In most cases, they are connected to either the Asian economic and political interests from abroad, or to real estate investment at home.

Chinatown residents registering to vote at a busy corner on Canal Street in Chinatown, New York, 1997. Since Chinatown residents tend to be new immigrants, they need to be educated about the American political process. It wasn't until the 1990s that local politicians began to court their votes. Photo © Corky Lee.

"Stop Anti-Asian Violence!" The Coalition to Commemorate Vincent Chin met in Confucius Plaza, New York City, in 1992 to mark the tenth anniversary of his death. In 1982, two unemployed white autoworkers from Detroit killed Vincent Chin, a young fifth-generation Chinese American, whom they took for a Japanese—and therefore blamed for the doldrums in Detroit's car industry. Their lenient sentence—three years' probation and a fine of $3,000—came to symbolize the collusion of the American justice system with white racist vigilantism. As a result, many Asian Americans came together in several new alliances, such as the American Citizens for Justice and the Coalition Against Anti-Asian Violence, to put pressure on the judiciary and law enforcement agencies to defend their rights. As instances of anti-Asian violence increased during the 1990s, every protest against the ineffectiveness of police in suppressing them evoked the case of Vincent Chin. Photo © Corky Lee.

UPTOWN/DOWNTOWN CHINESE AMERICANS

The new criteria for admission of immigrants to the United States, established by the Immigration Act of 1965, caused a rift between the Chinese admitted because their professional skills are needed in the United States economy and those who arrive simply to be reunited with their families.

The first group might best be described as the "Uptown Chinese"—well educated, they hold well-paying professional jobs, belong to the upper-middle class, and live in the suburbs, able to provide their children with the best educational opportunities. Most of them are not of Cantonese origin. They arrive in the United States already speaking English, but their native tongue is Mandarin.

The second group is comprised of the relatives of earlier immigrants from the rural regions of Canton. They are of humble background, poorly educated, and with minimal marketable skills. They usually end up living in the urban ethnic enclaves previously inhabited by their relatives, and might best be described as the "Downtown Chinese."

THE "UPTOWN CHINESE"

The success of the well-educated and upwardly mobile immigrant Chinese-American professionals in commanding high income and

(Opposite) **A new immigrant cools off on a rooftop in Old Chinatown, New York, with Manhattan's downtown skyline in the background. The symbols of America's wealth (Woolworth Building) and opportunity (The World Trade Center) continue to attract poor, rural immigrants from southern coastal China to the old Chinese neighborhood in their shadow. Photo ©1998 Chien-Chi Chang/ Magnum Photos.**

That's the Way To Go! The three Wu brothers, each one of them ranked first in his class at Harvard, with their parents in front of their family home in Flushing, New York, 1987. Children of highly educated professionals, immigrants from Taiwan, are encouraged at home to excel scholastically, an impressively large number of them attending the nation's most competitive colleges and universities. Photo © 1987 Patrick Zachman/Magnum Photos.

experiencing a relatively easy social integration prompted some observers in the 1980s to label Chinese Americans as "a model minority." Such an assessment, at first accepted by many with pride and appreciation, ended up being rather damning for the majority of Chinese Americans and injurious to their relations with other ethnic and racial groups. But above all, it was misleading.

The well-educated Chinese who started pouring into the United States after the passage of the Immigration Act of 1965, with its generous provisions for the admittance of highly skilled professionals, were by no means representative of ordinary, average Chinese anywhere—least of all the descendants of the Chinatown working class. They were in fact the "cream of the crop" of Taiwan's, Hong Kong's, and later, Mainland China's educational establishment, who often came to the United States with college degrees to attend graduate school at elite institutions. Their decision to remain in the United States epitomizes the post-World War II "brain drain" from Third World countries, which has emptied a score of poor developing nations of its most talented people and put them in the employ of the prospering economies of the Western world. These immigrants usually achieve upper-middle-class status very quickly upon arrival in the United States, because they enjoy easy access to the mainstream professional jobs in science, engineering, medicine, and education.

That this group of Chinese Americans enjoys an uncommonly privileged status is borne out by the fact that their median income is higher than that of average white Americans. But their level of education is also higher than that of average whites. Not only do a higher number of them attend college and graduate school; an even greater disproportionate number of them do so at the very best schools in the country. They have driven the statistics off the charts for Chinese Americans as a whole, who are conspicuously over-represented at the nation's best educational institutions: Chinese Americans, who are a mere 0.6 percent of the United States' population, represent 6 percent of the student body in colleges nationwide, and approximately 20 percent of the student body in ivy league schools and elite universities.

With a boutique on Madison Avenue in New York City, not far from where she was born, designer Vera Wang is the ultimate Chinese-American "uptown girl." Relaxing with her two daughters at home on Park Avenue is a rare but rewarding moment in the life of this super-achiever.

To a large degree this emphasis on education is a product of Chinese cultural heritage, but also of the belief of many minority immigrants that the only way for their children to attain social status is by being educated better than the majority. Such "Uptown Chinese" go to great lengths to meet this goal. One of their primary objectives is to move into affluent middle-class city neighborhoods and suburbs, but a major criterion for selecting the right locale is the quality of education in its school district. As a result, their offspring excel in academics. It is in this group of the American-born Uptown Chinese, who grow up rather privileged and whose drive to excel in school is highly encouraged, that one often finds winners of the prestigious Westinghouse Science Awards in disproportionate numbers. It is their achievements that have caught the attention of pollsters and media, bringing forth the idea of the "model minority."

Of course, the well-educated Chinese immigrants from this group have helped promote this idea, since they tend to attribute their rapid upward mobility to their cultural heritage. Once disparaging of the backward

Put Cheung, 17, with his algebraic structure project in New York, 1990. This young immigrant from Fuzhou, China, was a finalist in the 49th Westinghouse Science Talent Search in 1990. The pool of talented, well-performing young Chinese Americans has been expanding since the 1980s with the brain drain from mainland China.

aspects of Chinese culture in their countries of birth, they celebrate it in their suburban neighborhoods, which they now view as materialistic and creature-comfort oriented. The resurgence of their dormant "ethnic pride" is evident in the mushrooming of private Chinese-language schools all across the country. There are almost five hundred across the nation, ranging from a few that offer after-school instruction to immigrant children in poor Chinatown areas, to the many mostly weekend programs in affluent suburban neighborhoods, which bring in certified teachers from Taiwan and mainland China to teach Chinese-American children of all ages the basics of the official Chinese Mandarin dialect, elementary calligraphy, introduction to Chinese culture, and, occasionally, music. In the wider New York metropolitan area alone there are thirty-five such schools, spread across the suburbs of Long Island, Westchester County, and northern New Jersey.

Yet despite these unquestionable signs of success, the U.S. Census Bureau figures and the U.S. Commission on Civil Rights studies still indicate that Chinese Americans earn less than whites with equivalent levels of education and similar professional positions. One also hears persistent complaints from qualified Chinese who are regularly bypassed for promotions to management positions. It is a phenomenon dubbed by women and minority group members the "Glass Ceiling," and most Uptown Chinese who are

The Wong family grandfather watches over the children's school work, California, 1989. Photo © 1989 Alex Webb/ Magnum Photos. Education is emphasized in all Chinese-American families. Even children of recent working-class immigrants are expected to attend at least a community college.

(Following spread) A store clerk carefully weighs loose tea leaves and packs them to order at the Ten Ren Tea & Ginseng Company on Mott Street, the first Chinatown company in New York to specialize in selling high-quality loose-leaf teas from Asia. Prices vary from a few dollars to few hundred dollars a pound.

DARK   DARK   DARK

GREEN   GREEN   GREEN

Cooking School, Chinatown Manpower Project, New York, 1996. The cooking school was just one of several vocational training programs provided to new immigrants by the Manpower Project in 1996. The Project also teaches English as a second language, low-level clerical skills, and basic computer literacy. Its goal is to help new immigrants integrate into the American labor force, as well as to provide job retraining to low income people in the community. Photo © 1996 Chien-Chi Chang/ Magnum Photos.

clustered in the professions in science, engineering, medicine, and education seem to experience it at one time or another. Much more successful seem to be the Chinese Americans who work in smaller, independent companies, rather than in big corporations. (Or this might be just the question of perception. Successful white entrepreneurs also report more job satisfaction than white employees of large companies.) The most exceptional Chinese-American success stories have been high-performing venture companies in the field of artificial intelligence, like Wang Computers, Yahoo, Computer Associates, and hundreds of smaller Chinese-run firms in the Silicon Valley.

THE "DOWNTOWN CHINESE"

While the 1965 Immigration Act clearly favors professionals with skills needed in the United States, it reserves 74 percent of the immigration quota for the relatives of American citizens. Since most United States citizens of Chinese origin descend from humble families in the rural areas of southern China, their relatives typically have the same background. They are generally unskilled and do not speak English, so they tend to depend on their close family relations to survive. Because they usually settle in ethnic Chinese enclaves where they can find jobs, the old, dying Chinatowns have been suddenly revitalized by their arrival, and have expanded rapidly, well beyond their original size.

History of Chinatown. **Mural by Arthur Ho, Philadelphia, c. 1995. The mural depicts the key themes of the Chinese experience in America: the hard toil of early mine, railroad, and laundry workers, life in Chinatown, Chinatown redevelopment, and the current concerns of its residents: jobs, education, and the preservation of Chinatown heritage.**

A CLOSER LOOK:
NEW YEAR'S CELEBRATION

Traditional Chinese New Year is the most festive occasion in Chinese–American communities. Called "Spring Festival" in Chinese, it is the day that marks the beginning of the new planting season in the lunar agrarian calendar. More symbolically, it is the time of renewal and great joy in anticipation of better things to come: the house is cleaned the day before (it is inauspicious to leave anything old, stale, or spoiled sitting around), the family gathers on New Year's Eve for a meal to be shared with the ancestors (morsels of food are put on their altars), and, at midnight, the firecrackers are set to scare off the evil spirits so that the blessings and bounty of the new year can be ushered in without obstacles.

On New Year's Day steets in Chinatown explode with activity. Every storefront is decked out in red—which is the color for all joyous occasions in Chinese tradition; brides wear red for the traditional Chinese wedding ceremony. Red signs announcing "Happiness" and "Fortune" are put on the doors. Colorful processions headed by lion-dancers visit each business, door by door, bestowing good wishes and getting money-offerings in return. Every youth and martial arts group in the community puts on a lion dance as a way of raising funds for its annual activities. Every business generously contributes on this day. Give away money on this day—always wrapped in a red envelope—and riches will return to you manifold!

This is the day when one visits all members of the extended family, when every child gets a "little red wrapper" with money from all the relatives, and when traditional surname and village associations give their annual banquets for the entire membership with families. It is also the only day of the year when Chinatown businesses take a day off!

(Background) New Year on Mott Street, Chinatown, New York, 1991.
(Opposite) Chinese New Year, California Style: two men in lion
costumes ride in a convertible in San Francisco.

A fresh meat delivery on a snowy day, Chinatown, New York, 1996. New immigrants may be poor, but their taste for fresh meat, fruit, and vegetables is well catered to by Chinatown merchants who sell only fresh produce. Photo © 1996 Chien-Chi Chang/ Magnum Photos.

The Chinatown of New York's Manhattan borough is a good example of this phenomenon: it has burst through the seams of its original six city blocks and expanded to cover a thirty-block area in roughly twenty-five years. But this is not all. "Satellite" Chinatowns have sprouted throughout the metropolitan area, with major commercial centers in the boroughs of Queens (Flushing) and Brooklyn (Sunset Park). Several other outer-borough Chinatowns—Corona, Elmhurst, Woodside, Rego Park, Forest Hills, Sheepshead Bay, Bay Ridge, and Borough Park—are primarily residential. Queens and Brooklyn have in fact become the boroughs of choice for many new Chinese immigrants: in 1990, 65 percent of all Chinese residents of the New York metropolitan area residing in them (up from 28 percent in 1960).

Similar developments have occurred elsewhere in the country. Los Angeles, for instance, in addition to the old core Chinatown in the downtown area, now features new Chinatowns in Monterey Park, Alhambra, San Gabriel, Industry, El Monte, and Rosemead. Interestingly, many of these new

Bitter toil revisited, New York City, 1981. Whether in New York, California, or elsewhere in the country, late-20th century Chinatowns have something in common: they provide low-wage employment in industries that would have left the United States long ago if not for the cheap labor of new immigrants. In the garment industry, sweatshop conditions are a rule. Photo © Corky Lee.

Chinatowns have taken on the characteristics of typical American suburban sprawl. And perhaps not surprisingly, Monterey Park, Alhambra, and Rosemead were ranked among the top six destinations in the United States for the Chinese immigrating from Hong Kong, Taiwan, and mainland China between 1983 and 1990.

Whether in California, New York, or elsewhere in the country, these new Chinatowns all have something in common: they emerged in urban locations affected by deindustrialization and economic restructuring, where the tax base was declining and public services deteriorating, to provide employment in a "friendly environment" for the new immigrants. Capitalizing on the cheap labor of the new unskilled immigrants to resurrect dying and fleeing industries—the garment industry in particular—these ethnic Chinese enclaves quickly become economically viable, dynamic entities with thriving ethnic businesses and industries. Yet, despite their indubitable success in creating jobs in areas where the mainstream American businesses see no opportunities, and in attracting both overseas Chinese investment and outsourced jobs from larger domestic manufacturers, these enclaves can

Family Reunion, Chinatown, New York, 1989. A smiling 65-year-old restaurant worker reunites with his wife after 29 years of separation in his cramped tenement apartment. The photograph was taken to be sent to their children in China. Poor working-class immigrants today still live in Chinatown tenements and "bachelor apartments" of yore, in conditions that haven't changed much over the generations. (Pictures of George Washington and his Chinese equivalent, Dr. Sun Yat-sen, hang on the wall.) Photo © Corky Lee.

be traps. They may seem "friendly" at first to the immigrants who do not speak English, but they leave the employees vulnerable to the whims of owners and employers. Low-wage sweatshop conditions abound. The new immigrants work long hours (twelve and even fifteen hours a day is not unusual), often more than six days a week, for less than the minimum wage and no benefits. They live in typical crowded ghetto tenements, served by poor school systems, and seemingly unprotected by the enforcers of American laws. How can they be so utterly neglected by the mainstream American institutions?

Since the new immigrant communities lack voting power, they are of no real interest to most mainstream American political institutions and law enforcement agencies. Rather like the old Chinatowns during the period of Chinese Exclusion, these new ethnic enclaves, too, are left to fend for themselves in a continuous condition of self-rule. This unregulated environment has encouraged many Chinatown employers to push the working standards further down by hiring illegal Chinese immigrants.

Although illegal immigration is by no means a new or exclusively Chinese phenomenon, public attention in the United States has certainly been caught by several failed large-scale attempts at illegal entry into the country by boatloads of Chinese during the 1980s and 1990s. One of the more spectacular cases, which unfolded live on local TV in 1993 was the *Golden Venture* incident where hundreds of exhausted stowaways waded or floated toward shore and drowned in frigid waters off Rockaway Beach, while stunned Americans watched. Many spectators could not help but feel admiration for the determination of these pitiable would-be immigrants. But public sympathy has its limits, as this was merely one among many similar incidents.

The wave of illegal Chinese immigrants washing onto American shores is the direct result of China's rapid economic development since the mid-1980s, in which Chinese society suffered tremendous social dislocations. Millions of people roam around China looking for jobs, while the

most adventuresome among them have joined an exodus of people seeking their fortunes abroad. Their venturesome undertaking comes at an incredible cost: emigrants from China pay between U.S. $30,000 and $40,000 in fees to the smugglers who bring them illegally into the United States. They can usually borrow enough money from their relatives to put together a deposit of $1,000 to $1,500 to start the trip. The rest they pay back, with interest, once they arrive in the United States and start working. Many unscrupulous employers are eager to employ them since, pressed by debts and lacking legal status, they are forced to work for practically nothing—by American standards, that is. Many of them still maintain that they are glad to be in the United States, because of future opportunities for their children.

Illegally smuggled immigrants from China have fueled the creation of thousands of sweatshops in New York and California and in the process have caused problems for the legal immigrants. Because of their presence in the American job market, many legal working-class immigrants from China are forced to work for substandard wages. During the 1990s the legal immi-

"We Must Go To America!" Boatloads of illegal immigrants from mainland China have been arriving regularly on American shores, ever since the Chinese government relaxed its economic and emigration policies in the early 1980s. Only a handful of them are apprehended at the border. This unfortunate group, under tow by the Coast Guard cutter *Conifer,* arrived in San Diego, California, aboard the *Sung Li #6,* on July 11, 1993. On the same day, 659 other illegal would-be immigrants were aboard three ships off the coast of Baja, California.

A CLOSER LOOK:
GOLDEN VENTURE

The name of the infamous 42-year old cargo steamer that ran aground at Rockaway Beach in Queens, New York, on June 6, 1993, could not have been more ironically chosen. Its 286 passengers had been living on little more than rice and water in its rusty, fetid hold for almost four months while being transported illegally from mainland China—a privilege for which each one of them was to pay $30,000 to their smugglers once they reached the United States. As *Golden Venture*'s bow dug into a sandbar with a lurch, its exhausted and dazed human cargo was discharged into the chilly pre-dawn waters of the Atlantic. By daybreak, ten of the illegal passengers had drowned, while the U.S. Coast Guard sent in small craft and helicopters to rescue others who were wading toward shore, right into the spotlight of the waiting television crews. The ordeal of the *Golden Venture* passengers turned into a national obsession, with the public divided between those who admired the determination and pioneering spirit of the would-be immigrants, while others saw them as a symbol of an alien, illegal invasion of America's borders threatening domestic jobs and security.

Illegal immigration into the United States is a big problem indeed, and it is usually dealt with inadequately by temporary detention and deportations at the border. The *Golden Venture* passengers were incarcerated for several years, but they continued to captivate the American public by proving that their enterprising spirit could not be restrained: they used toilet paper, magazine pages, newspaper, cardboard, markers, and glue—all materials readily available in prison—to express their experience and yearnings through a unique form of "folk art."

From the *Fly to Freedom* exhibit at the Museum of Chinese in the Americas: (*Above right*) **Dragon;** (*right*) **Goldfish;** (*opposite*) **Eagle. Just some of the remarkable objects made of "found" materials created by the passengers of the *Golden Venture* during their imprisonment.**

Martial arts star Bruce Lee in the 1973 film, *Enter the Dragon*. Bruce Lee is the first American-born Chinese known to, literally, the whole world (although, ironically, many people think of him as Chinese). His success was phenomenal because he came to symbolize the triumph of the "little guy" to boys everywhere—America, Asia, Europe, Africa, and Australia. He single-handedly spawned a global martial arts industry, and is still revered by thousands of fan clubs on all continents even more than a quarter of a century after his death.

grants have also increasingly experienced reduced benefits, public scrutiny, and anti-immigrant animosity.

AMERICAN-BORN CHINESE

Statistically, American-born Chinese exhibit the traits of the "model minority," as they have been dubbed. They are more successful occupationally: 77 percent of them hold white-collar jobs, compared to 59 percent of the white population. Almost twice as many American-born Chinese Americans are involved in professional occupations as white Americans. In this they are quite different from the foreign-born Chinese Americans, whose occupational patterns reflect the duality of the post-1965 immigrant groups, and who can be found clustered both in high-paying professional and managerial positions and low-paying service jobs, with relatively few representatives in between. The foreign-born Chinese Americans are, therefore, also more likely than white Americans to be employed as waiters, dishwashers, and in other service occupations in hotels and restaurants.

What this means is that the American-born Chinese are still strongly influenced by their parents' values, which stress education as a way to move upward in society. Even children from working-class families are encouraged to attend at least community colleges and major in practical fields such as computer technology, business management, accounting, library science, or nursing. The children from professional families are expected to do better than their parents, who frequently feel that they sacrificed much for their children's future by coming to the United States.

Los Angeles–born playwright David Henry Hwang won acclaim for his early 1980s off-Broadway plays (*F.O.B.*, *The Dance and the Railroad*, *Family Devotions*), which explored the complexities of being Chinese in America. His best-known Broadway play, *M. Butterfly*, received many nominations (Pulitzer Prize) and awards (most notably, the Outer Critics Circle Award and Drama Desk Award). © 1996 Lia Chang Gallery.

The American-born Chinese often experience problems in their formative years, because they are torn between the more liberal mainstream American values and their Asian parents' more restrictive ones. They are often forced into practical fields in which they have no interest, enrolled in various supplementary classes and educational activities rather than sports, and subjected to strict discipline at home. Their parents tend to closely monitor their social circles, and restrict them as they see fit. Because of strong family pressure to succeed, those who do not do well are often made to feel like outcasts or failures.

Of course, most do rather well. According to the 1990 census, 41 percent of Chinese Americans had completed four or more years of college, compared to less than 22 percent of the white population; the numbers were even more striking when it came to postgraduate and professional degrees: some 19.1 percent of the Chinese-American population had them, compared to 7.7 percent of the whites. But such success often comes at a high cost in terms of personal and professional gratification. Also, despite the high proportion of Chinese Americans in the professions, they are often absent from executive, supervisory, and decision-making positions, and they are paid considerably less than comparably qualified whites. First, American-born Chinese are more likely to question this incongruity than their foreign-born parents. They are also more likely to respond to signs of racism by reaffirming their ethnic and racial identity, unlike their parents, who most of the time see assimilation as the best way to cope with their problems. This often results in a cultural tug of war, as different forces claim them as Asian Americans, as Chinese Americans, as members of a model minority or as, simply, Americans.

American-born Chinese became increasingly ethnically conscious during the 1980s and 1990s. They joined other Asians in demanding Asian-American Studies programs at universities around the country. They tend to socialize with other Asian Americans. They belong to Asian social clubs. There is even an all-Chinese dancing club in New York City, which holds regular dancing events in rented trendy dance halls and manages to fill them to capacity. The more verbally inclined publish Asian-American maga-

zines—both stylish glossies and smart on-line magazines—where they project positive images of Asians and Chinese Americans. This new crop of Chinese Americans is gaining high visibility. They are well-educated, financially comfortable, sophisticated in taste, and savvy about their own potential as consumers highly sought after by advertisers. They have taken the bull by the horns.

The other segment of the American-born Chinese population is well integrated into American society and chooses to completely identify with mainstream America. A significant number of people in this group enter into interracial marriages—about one-third of all American-born Chinese Americans on the average, and about 40 percent of the women.

(Above) "Super Chinks' perform at the Asian Pacific American Heritage Festival, Union Square, New York City, August 1998. This unique Chinese-American rap group from New York does not shy from shocking its audiences. Their songs are provocative; their style the ultimate "downtown cool." Photo © Corky Lee.

(Following spread) Mott Street, the heart of New York's Old Chinatown, by night.

197

RX

中華西藥房

PHARMACY
65

敘樂飯店
RESTAURANT

CELEBRATES
OUNDING OF REPUBLIC OF CHINA

天華閣
mandarin
court
restaurant
61

RX

中華西藥房

PHARMACY
65

大田飯店
HONG RESTAURANT

T&H IMPORTS

JOY LUCK
RESTAURANT

Häagen-Dazs
ICE CREAM

CHINESE-AMERICAN WOMEN

The perception of what it means to be a Chinese-American woman is easily shaped by the sophisticated image projected to the American public by top media personalities like Connie Chung and Kaity Tong, by the celebrated fashion designer Vera Wang who outfits many Hollywood stars on Academy Award night, and by influential writers like Amy Tan and Maxine Hong Kingston. There is no doubt that Chinese women in America have come a long way from the early days of Chinese immigration, when the *Daily Alta California* referred to them as "queer and diminutive specimens of the human family, bunched up in bandanna 'kerchiefs,' wearing blue shirts and big unmentionables, walking through the streets with as much delicacy as a turkey treading on hot ashes," (August 17, 1852). Or that they no longer have to suffer the indignity of the first Chinese woman known to have come to America, Afong Moy, who was imported by an American entrepreneur in 1834 among other "Oriental showpieces" as an object of curiosity, and who was exhibited in New York as "a Chinese lady in native costume" to show "New York belles how different ladies look in widely separated regions." She reportedly "charmed audiences in Manhattan and Brooklyn in 1834 and 1835," and her capacity to attract attention was so significant that a few years later Barnum's Chinese Museum exhibited another Chinese woman, Pwan Yekoo, as "a genuine Chinese lady ... prepared to exhibit her charming self, her curious retinue, and her fairy feet (only two and a half

(Opposite) **Maxine Hong Kingston, in Berkeley, California, on May 18, 1994, on the opening night of *The Woman Warrior*—the stage production of her book *The Woman Warrior: Memoirs of a Girlhood Among Ghost*. The book, which won her the National Book Critics Circle Award for nonfiction in 1976, describes her childhood in a Chinese immigrant family and is considered a classic of Asian-American literature. © 1994 Lia Chang Gallery.**

inches long), to an admiring and novelty-loving public" (*The New York Times*, April 21, 1850).

Young Chinese-American women today talk in an Asian-American Internet publication of growing up suspicious that they are attractive to males of mainstream society, which they generally aspire to join, merely for being different or exotic. They also talk about the complex problem of living in a male-dominated American society while having to cope with their even more oppressively male-dominated Asian families. Some escape it by marrying out of their ethnic and racial group, which, many find, is the easiest way to distance themselves from their Chinese family pressures. Forty percent of Chinese-American women marry out of their race. A conspicuously large number of the most accomplished among them marry Jewish men. Others have rejected marriage and child-bearing altogether, opting for career success instead. Many have linked up with other

Attorney General Janet Reno poses for a photograph with actress-cum-photojournalist Lia Chang at the Asian Pacific American Heritage Month Reception in Washington, D.C., May 9, 1996. © 1996 Lia Chang Gallery.

Asian-American women, with whom they share many experiences and concerns, to form Asian-American women's organizations and support groups of various kinds.

Chinese-American women are generally more politically active than the average Chinese-American male. Many can be found directing social-welfare agencies, heading non-profit organizations, acting as leaders in education reform and promoters of health clinics and day-care centers. Even in the working-class families among the new immigrants, because of the largely marginalized status of the non-English-speaking Chinese male in American society at large, it is often the women who assume the leading role in the household: as wives, mothers, family planners, primary income earners, health-care providers, and decision makers. In that sense, they are following in the tradition of early immigrant women from China. Contrary to the stereotype of the stay-at-home housewife, these Chinese women usually had to work alongside their husbands, because the Chinese were forced into small, family-run, low-income, labor-intensive occupations like

The New Face of Law Enforcement in Chinatown, New York City, 1995. With the affirmative action programs established in the wake of the civil rights movement, Chinatown women were able to enter an array of professions that were previously closed to them. Photo © 1995 Lia Chang Gallery.

farming, gardening, restaurant ownership, and laundering, which could only survive if the whole family worked. At the same time, of course, Chinese women were expected to perform all the domestic chores.

Despite the proverbial Asian preference for male offspring and relative conservatism when it comes to rearing girls, Chinese-American women are much better educated than white women according to statistics (29.5 percent of them have college degrees, compared to 13.3 percent of white women). Consequently, their average income is also higher than that of white women. And, although in terms of personal income they lag behind both white men and Asian-American men in comparable positions, a large proportion of Chinese-American women work as newscasters, doctors, attorneys, entrepreneurs, and business executives.

Television journalist Connie Chung, with her husband, Maury Povich, attending a party given by the gossip-columnist Liz Smith on January 8, 1992. Marriages between high-powered Chinese-American women and Jewish men are not uncommon.

(*Above*) Scene from the movie *The Joy Luck Club,* released in 1993. A story of four Chinese women who immigrated to America, and their four assimilated American-born daughters who learn to appreciate the old quaint ways. Featuring an almost all-Asian-American cast, Hong-Kong-born American-trained director Wayne Wang, Amy Tan as screenwriter, and Janet Young as one of the producers, this is truly "the" Asian-American Hollywood film with no rival.

(*Right*) Amy Tan in Dallas, Texas, on September 15, 1993, at the opening of the movie *The Joy Luck Club,* based on her best-selling first novel of the same title. Two of her other titles, *The Kitchen God's Wife* and *The Hundred Secret Senses*, are equally well received by the critics and the public.

(*Following spread*) A movie still from the 1993 Samuel Goldwyn release, *The Wedding Banquet*, starring (left to right) May Chin, Ah-leh Guo, Mitchell Lichtenstein, Sihung Lung, and Winston Chao. The film's Chinese-American screenwriter/producer/director, Taiwanese-born Ang Lee, explores a culture clash between his native and adopted countries.

A CLOSER LOOK:
FASHION

In the 1990s a profusion of Chinese designers exploded onto the American fashion scene and became household names. Some are American-born (Anna Sui, Vera Wang); others came from China, Taiwan, Hong Kong (Vivienne Tam, pictured), and even Malaysia (Yeohlee, pictured). The most visible ones have their own name-brand boutiques on Madison Avenue and in the Soho district of New York City—the place to be in the fashion Mecca of the world. Others, like Galinda Wang, the founder of La Chine Classics, which produces inexpensive blouses for the mass market, have quietly built multi-million dollar empires by catering to more mainstream tastes. In terms of understanding and influencing those mainstream tastes, and developing strategies to reach out to a broad base of return customers, two "older" Chinese-American clothing companies, Bugle Boy (founded by Bill Mow in 1976) and Nautica (founded by David Chu in 1983) are the ones to beat in year 2000.

(Opposite left) Yeohlee, at the official site of the press fashion shows in Bryant Park, New York 1997. © 1997 Lia Chang Gallery.

(Opposite right) A model in a dress by the New York-based Chinese-born designer Han Feng at the Bryant Park fashion shows, October 1995. © 1995 Lia Chang Gallery.

(Right) Vivienne Tam's Mao Dresses, on display at the Fashion Institute of Technology exhibit called *China Chic*, in April 1999. © 1999 Lia Chang Gallery.

(Below) Vivienne Tam in front of her Green Street Boutique, in Soho, New York, 1998. Photo © Corky Lee.

ARRIVED AT LONG LAST

The rising economic power of Taiwan, Hong Kong, and mainland China has caused many Americans to show greater interest in all things Chinese and to view Chinese Americans with increased respect. One can almost say that a kind of "Asian chic" has emerged in American society, as a result of the Asian economic success and the growing interconnectedness of Asian and American economies. Booming United States–China trade has given enormous opportunities to Americans of Chinese descent to work as intermediaries between the two countries, and has encouraged others to become the conveyers of Chinese arts, culture, and science to increasingly curious and receptive American audiences. With the growing contacts between the two cultures, exhibitions of classical and contemporary Chinese visual art, and even performances of the less accessible forms of traditional Chinese opera have become quite common in America. In 1998 and 1999, several leading museums in the country mounted ground-breaking shows of both traditional and contemporary Chinese art, much of which is produced on American soil by expatriate, "globalist," and Chinese-American artists who call New York home. Many American artists experiment with traditional Chinese techniques and forms.

Mainstream American lifestyles are increasingly influenced by things Chinese. Not only are a huge proportion of cheap consumer goods routinely used in everyday life made in China; most Americans cannot remem-

(Previous spread) **A movie still from the 1993 Samuel Goldwyn release, *The Wedding Banquet*, starring (left to right) May Chin, Ah-leh Guo, Mitchell Lichtenstein, Sihung Lung, and Winston Chao. The film's Chinese-American screenwriter/producer/ director, Taiwanese-born Ang Lee, explores a culture clash between his native and adopted countries.**

(Opposite) **Cellist Yo-Yo Ma is a virtuoso without equal in the music world today. Since his first public recital in Paris at age six and his concert at Carnegie Hall at age nine, he has played with numerous symphony orchestras around the world, and won eight Grammy Awards for his unique interpretations of the classical repertoire, as well as for his inspired forays into contemporary music and jazz.**

Professor David D. Ho, M.D., is the Scientific Director of the Aaron Diamond AIDS Research Center at The Rockefeller University in New York. He is best known for developing a "cocktail" of antiviral drugs that successfully inhibit the HIV virus in the early stages of infection—an achievement for which he was named "Man of the Year" in 1995 by *Time* magazine.

ber the time when their everyday dietary options did not include take-out from that ubiquitous neighborhood Chinese restaurant. Chinese martial arts continue to be popular despite the premature death of the all-time favorite martial arts movie star, American-born Bruce Lee. A growing number of Americans are turning to Chinese herbal medicine and acupuncture for health problems, and to enhance their well-being and performance on the job, in sports, and at play. New herbal-based pharmaceutical and nutritional supplement companies mushroomed in the United States during the 1980s and 1990s, making herbal nutrition, cosmetics, and medicine one of the fastest-growing industries of the period.

Only a few decades earlier, most of the Chinese in America, if they gained any prominence at all, were engaged in technical and scientific pursuits. Now, Chinese Americans are making rapid advances on a number of fronts. To be sure, many still occupy critical positions within the American scientific establishment—at leading universities, elite research labs, and major corporate science divisions. Their contributions in the fields of super-conductivity, artificial intelligence, biochemistry, and immunology have been significant. The scientific director of the Aaron Diamond AIDS Research Center at The Rockefeller University, David Ho, the creator of the potent "cocktail" of three antiviral drugs to be used in the early stages of the HIV infection, was named "Man of the Year" by *Time* magazine in 1995. Paul C.W. Chu, Director of the Texas Center for Superconductivity and T.L.L. Temple Chair of Science at the University of Houston, is a member of the National Academy of Sciences and the American Academy of Arts and Sciences, and has received numerous awards for his work on superconductivity, including the National Medal of Science.

Professor Steven Chu (shown in his laboratory at Stanford University) was a co-recipient of the Nobel Prize for Physics in 1997, "for development of methods to cool and trap atoms with laser light." Five other Chinese-American scientists received the Nobel Prize: four for physics, and one for chemistry.

Then there are the Nobel Prize winners: beginning with Franklin Chen Ning Yang and Tsung-dao Lee, joint winners of the Nobel Prize for Physics in 1957, for their work on parity laws and elementary particles, and continuing with Samuel C.C. Ting, co-recipient of the Nobel Prize for Physics in 1976, for "pioneering work in the discovery of a heavy elementary par-

Architect Maya Lin began her exceptional career by winning a national competition to design the Vietnam War Memorial in Washington, D.C., in 1981, while still a senior at Yale University. Here, she displays the model for the memorial.

ticle of a new kind"; Yuan T. Lee, co-recipient of the Nobel Prize for Chemistry in 1986, "for contributions concerning the dynamics of chemical elementary processes"; Steven Chu, co-recipient of the Nobel Prize for Physics in 1997, "for development of methods to cool and trap atoms with laser light"; and Daniel C. Tsui, co-recipient of the Nobel Prize for Physics in 1998, "for discovery of a new form of quantum fluid with fractionally charged excitations."

While celebrated for their discoveries in the scientific community, the Nobel Prize winners are probably not as well known to the general public as the Chinese-American architects whose work is, by its nature, much more visible. The world-famous I.M. Pei was born in China, but has lived in the United States since the mid-1930s when he came to study architecture at the Massachusetts Institute of Technology, and has been a United States citizen since 1954. His architectural designs have won many awards, including the highest architectural honor in the United States, The American Institute of Architects Gold Medal, in 1979, and the prestigious Pritzker Prize in 1983, "for having given this century some of its most beautiful interior spaces and exterior forms." Indeed, some of the most stunning and controversial buildings in the world bear Pei's signature use of geometric shapes and audacity: the Bank of China in Hong Kong; the

National Center of Atmospheric Research in Boulder, Colorado; the East Building of the National Gallery of Art in Washington, D.C.; the Miho Museum of Shiga, Japan; and the best-known of them all, the Pyramid Court at the Louvre in Paris. When it opened in 1993 after more than a decade of hostile anticipation and advance criticism, it won accolades. "Of all the *Grands Projets* in Paris," as Dennis Sharp wrote in *Twentieth Century Architecture: A Visual History*, "none created such a stir as the Pei Pyramids in the courtyard of the famous Louvre Museum. Spectacular in concept and form, they provide a startling reminder of the audacious ability of modern architects to invigorate and recirculate traditional architectural forms."

Another Chinese-American architect has caught the public attention with her bold vision and innovative, often controversial designs on a scale simi-

(Left) **Architect Maya Lin is warmly congratulated by fellow Doctor of Arts honoree, philanthropist Walter Annenberg, at Harvard University's commencement, 1996.**

(Following spread) **Chinese-American architect I. M. Pei. Born in Guangzhou, China, in 1917, he came to the United States to study architecture at the Massachusetts Institute of Technology in 1935, and stayed on to become one of the most prominent members of the new Chinese elite in America. He is shown seated in front of his sketch for the East Wing of the National Gallery in Washington, D.C.—one of his landmark contributions to American architecture.**

"Yahoo!" indeed. Jerry Yang displays a million-dollar smile— make that a billion. No, make that three billion (and rising), for the 10 percent share Jerry holds in the company he co-founded with David Filo in 1994, while still an engineering student at Stanford University. The two were called "yahoos" for thinking of making a business out of internet site listings. Whoever thought of calling them "yahoos" can think again.

lar to I.M. Pei's. Maya Lin stunned the world when, as a twenty-one-year- old senior at Yale University in 1981, she won a national competition to design the Vietnam Veterans Memorial in Washington, D.C. She conceived her design as a park within a park—a quiet, protected place that was a sanctuary unto itself, yet harmonized with the overall plan of Constitution Gardens. To achieve that effect, she chose polished black granite for the walls. Their mirror-like surface reflects the images of the surrounding trees, lawns, and monuments. The walls point to the Washington Monument and Lincoln Memorial, thus bringing the Vietnam Memorial into the historical context of our country. The names of Americans who died in the war are inscribed in the chronological order of their deaths, showing the war as a series of individual sacrifices and giving each name a special place in history. Visitors are invited to touch the names. The response of the daily visitors to the monument, particularly of the war veterans, has been overwhelming. Another one of Lin's remarkable, monumental designs is the Civil Rights Memorial in Montgomery, Alabama. Here, too, visitors are invited to touch the names of the dead engraved in a circular black granite table, and some reportedly weep, their tears falling into the water that emerges from the table's center and joins the cascade over a curved black granite wall behind the table on which Martin Luther King, Jr.'s words, ". . . until justice rolls down like waters and righteousness like a mighty stream," are engraved.

Other Chinese Americans are shaping the contemporary life in the United States in less striking, but perhaps even more effective ways. Many of the ground-breaking computer-related technologies and products, such as computer hardware and software, memory modules, integrated circuits, telecom components, fiber optics products, remote-access security products, imaging systems, communication devices for the handicapped, and remote video-conferencing systems have been developed and marketed by a slew of Chinese-American companies that cropped up in the 1990s. Computer Associates International Inc., Gemstar International Ltd., Proton Corporation, Supercom Inc., Diamond Multimedia, Quantex Microsystems Inc., and the highly recognizable Yahoo! Inc., which provides directories and the most popular search engine for the World Wide Web, are merely the leading Chinese-American-owned companies among the so-called "high-tech titans," who are shaping the future of the Silicon Valley, California, the United States of America, and the world beyond. Four hundred electronics companies in the Silicon Valley are owned by Asian Americans, many of them Chinese. The Asian Business League of Silicon Valley and the Asian American Manufacturers Association of Northern California—two business networks set up in the early 1980s to provide a network of mutual support for Asian-American entrepreneurs—promise to deliver "unimagined new software and wonder drugs, Web servers and computer games, networking hardware and storage devices at a rate the present regime" in those industries "can't fully digest," proclaims the Asian-American Supersite, goldsea.com, on the Web.

"The Gold Rush of 2000 belongs to Asian Americans." Once stereotyped as being very good at technological things but unable to manage, Chinese Americans are proving that they can make sound busi-

David Chu, co-founder, president, and design director of Nautica Enterprises Inc., photographed in 1995. The "cool" design of his quality men's sportswear is only a part of his success. Marketing through hip advertising, dozens of "factory" outlets in the United States, and international licensing of the company trademark has made David Chu one of the twenty wealthiest Asians in America. © 1995 Lia Chang Gallery.

(Below left) **WNBC reporter Ti-Hua Chang, one of the first Chinese-American men to break into channel-network primetime news, at ease on the rooftop of his Manhattan apartment, 1996. © 1996 Lia Chang Gallery.**

(Below right) **Yan Can Cook—"So can you!" exclaims Martin Yan, author of a popular 1990s television show that teaches Chinese cooking to American audiences. His cooking skills are amazing; his enthusiasm infectious.**

ness decisions and run prosperous businesses. They have proven most successful when self-employed in cutting-edge high-tech industries—particularly in California, where the hardiest and most entrepreneurial among them are finally positioned to reap the full benefits of sticking it out against all odds in order to achieve that elusive, long-delayed American dream.

Bio-technology is another cutting-edge high-tech industry that can provide entrepreneurial visionaries with a chance of spectacular financial success. As in the computer industry, here, too, the technology has allowed entire industries to spring up, with savvy individuals taking leadership roles. Although a lot of Chinese Americans work in the biological sciences, very few have been involved in the managerial side, but the astonishing success of James Kuo, the thirty-two-year-old CEO of Discovery Laboratories Inc., nicknamed the "biotech golden boy," for creating some of today's hottest biotech companies in just a few years, promises to open the door to

other ambitious young Asians in the field. Then there is Cyrus Tang, the founder, chairman, and CEO of Tang Industries. He is a reclusive, self-made billionaire, whose umbrella corporation includes businesses engaged in areas as diverse as metal fabrication, pharmaceuticals, and office furniture. He is ranked second on the list of America's top one hundred Asian entrepreneurs, on which roughly 90 percent of those listed are Chinese Americans. Among them, in addition to the "high-tech titans," one also finds Bill Mow, the founder, chairman, and CEO of Bugle Boy Industries, and David Chu, co-founder, president, and design director of Nautica Enterprises Inc.—both extremely successful designers, manufacturers, and retailers of men's sportswear; Vera Wang, the famous designer of high fashion, and other lesser known names who have made their mark in herbal foods, cosmetics, and household products, water-contamination control, national distribution of Asian foods, golf courses, Chinese take-out and other chain restaurants, retail banking, investment fund management, ship repair and environmental services, biotech kits, and therapies for HIV, asthma, and allergies.

Labeled "designer to the stars," Vera Wang opened her first boutique in Manhattan in 1990, and has no formal design training. As many other Chinese Americans of her generation, she was not allowed to go to art school by her parents, who wanted her to concentrate on more "practical subjects."

Chen Chi in his studio at The National Arts Club in Gramercy Park, New York City. One of the first visual artists from China to successfully bridge the Eastern and Western traditions in his work. Upon arrival in the United States in 1947, he developed a uniquely contemporary, yet tradition-based watercolor style (see his watercolor in the front of this book). His work has been shown in numerous art museums, including the Metropolitan Museum of Art, the Whitney Museum of American Art, the National Academy of Design, and the Smithsonian Institution.

Chinese Americans are increasingly making great strides in the arts and humanities, sports, and entertainment fields. Writers such as Maxine Hong Kingston, Amy Tan, and Frank Chin are well known to millions of readers, not just in the United States but worldwide. In the news media, the sight of a Chinese face on a TV newscast is no longer a novelty, with Connie Chung still leading the way, while newspaper journalists like Sheryl WuDunn of *The New York Times* and Ying Chan of *The New York Daily News* win national rewards for their reporting, and Catherine Shen quietly publishes the *Honolulu Star Bulletin*. In the theater, David Henry Hwang has won several awards, including a Tony and an Obie, for his plays produced both on and off Broadway, while Ming Cho Lee's theatrical set designs have for decades provided dramatic backdrops for productions of Joseph Papp's New York Shakespeare Festival, the American Ballet Theatre, Joffrey Ballet, and the Metropolitan and San Francisco Operas. Once relegated to roles as villains or comical characters in the American film industry, Chinese Americans today are engaged in all aspects of film production: James Wong Howe is a celebrated cinematographer whose movies include *Body and Soul* and *Sweet Smell of Success*; director Ang Lee has received foreign language Academy Award nominations for his films, *The Wedding Banquet* and *Eat, Drink, Man Woman*; Chris Lee is president of production at Columbia TriStar Pictures; and there are several actresses and actors whose faces are recognizable to American audiences nationwide, such as Joan Chen, and B.D. Wong. Add to these notables the famous musicians such as the cellist Yo-Yo Ma and the violinist Cho-Liang Lin, and the sports stars such as the tennis player Michael Chang, or the ice skaters Michelle Kwan and Tiffany Chin, and the list of Chinese-American role models in just about every walk of life is complete.

Indeed, as the prominence of such ethnic role models grows, young second generation Chinese Americans are slowly being allowed by their parents to enter more diverse fields. Throughout the 1990s, an ever-growing number of Chinese-American students have been attending the Fashion Institute of Technology, Pratt Institute's School of Arts and Design and School of Architecture, film schools at New York University and the University of California at Los Angeles, and numerous music schools. More than half of the students at New York's prestigious Julliard School of Music are of

Cinematographer James Wong Howe, during filming of the movie-classic, *Body and Soul*—one of the top ten movies of 1947. Best known for his work on the film *Sweet Smell of Success,* Wong Howe was one of the first Chinese Americans to achieve national prominence in the arts.

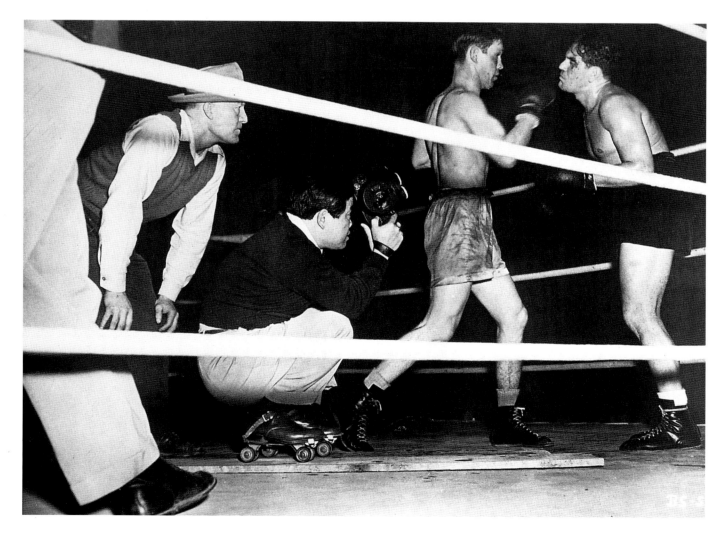

A "Good Luck" Buddhist Ceremony on the first day of production on the set of *Siao Yu*, produced by Ang Lee (the acclaimed director of *The Wedding Banquet, Ice Storm,* and *Sense and Sensibility*; standing in the left corner of the photograph), and directed by Sylvia Chang (second from right), in Columbus Park, Chinatown, New York, October 6, 1994. © 1994 Lia Chang Gallery.

Asian descent, and a significant percentage are Chinese Americans. At other colleges, an ever-increasing number can be found majoring in humanities, social sciences, and law. Many Chinese-American graduates of the Yale Law School and Harvard's Kennedy School of Government and Public Policy are already deeply steeped in American mainstream politics and policy making.

One of the most unexpected achievements of Chinese Americans during the last two decades of the twentieth century has been the growth of their political participation and representation. Asian Americans in general tend to be typecast as politically inactive, and particularly passive when it comes to suffering abuse at the hands of their employers. That myth is slowly beginning to shatter.

Rank-and-file activism among working-class Chinese immigrants has become quite common. In 1982, twenty thousand Chinese Gimbernat ladies joined an International Ladies Garment Workers Union (ILGWU) demonstration in New York, demanding that Chinese contractors sign a union contract. Nobody was more surprised by the turnout than the union itself. Historically, all too many American labor unions have shown a racist attitude when it comes to the Chinese. But, with or without the support of

American organized labor, Chinese-American workers have been organizing steadily. With the growing number of Asian immigrants joining the American working class, Asian membership in trade unions is also increasing, and one of the tactics employed by Asian activists is to form new Asian chapters in order to pressure the unions into representing the interests of Asian workers.

There are also a number of independent labor organizations that represent exclusively the interests of Chinese workers. One of the most successful grassroots labor organizations has been the Chinese Staff and Workers Association, initially formed to represent Chinese restaurant workers in New York, and to encourage the ILGWU to fight against Chinatown sweatshops. More recently, the association has also supported the attempts of Chinese immigrant workers to penetrate the trades previously closed to them—particularly the construction industry. Other grassroots political organizations, such as the Asian American Legal Defense and Education

Washington State Senator Gary Locke, with his wife, fundraising in Chinatown, New York, 1997. Photo © Corky Lee.

A CLOSER LOOK:
A. MAGAZINE: INSIDE ASIAN AMERICA

With a bimonthly circulation of 180,000 the *A. Magazine* is the largest publication for English-speaking Asian Americans in the country. It was founded in 1989 by Harvard graduate Jeff Yang (*inset picture below right*) to cater to the growing group of young, well-educated, and sophisticated American-born Asian Americans, who are content to be defined by the mainstream society and media as "the other." These image-savvy and increasingly assertive young Chinese Americans have taken into their own hands the task of projecting themselves onto the American cultural screen.

Now and Again:
Actor Russell Wong

Fund, the Organization of Chinese Americans, the Chinese American Action Committee, and Chinese for Affirmative Action, also aim at helping the new immigrants better integrate themselves into the American working class.

On the other end of the economic scale, prosperous Chinese-American professionals have penetrated electoral politics and have increasingly been able to attain prominent elective positions. As lieutenant governor of Delaware, S.B. Woo was, in 1983, one of the first Chinese Americans to successfully run for public office in a state where no more than two thousand members of the electorate were Chinese. Other visible elected officials of recent years have been Washington State Governor Gary Locke, U.S. Deputy Attorney General Bill Lan Lee, and Oregon Congressman David Wu.

(Above left) **Can't Jump? Tennis player Michael Chang, as the first Chinese-American tennis player to break into the top ten on the ATP tour rankings (a ranking he held for seven years), he serves as a role model for many young Asian-American would-be athletes.**

(Above right) **The 1998 Winter Olympic Games Silver medallist in women's figure skating, Michelle Kwan is known for her outstanding grace and artistry. A top contender since the age of 13, she does not plan to quit until she brings home Olympic gold.**

Visual artist Xu Bing is one of many Chinese-trained artists who now call New York home. Just a dozen years out of art school, he has captured the attention of the international art world with his bold, innovative installations, shown as often in Venice, London, Madrid, Ottawa, or Mallorca, as in New York (solo exhibition at the New Museum of Contemporary Art, 1998; Banner Project, MOMA, 1999). He is the 1999 recipient of the MacArthur Foundation's Fellowship Program Award (the "Genius Award").

A FINAL NOTE

Once the only ethnic group to be specifically targeted by immigration laws for exclusion from the United States of America, Chinese in America now find themselves with every reason to be proud of their heritage, and with even more reason to celebrate the persistence of their forebears in refusing to be denied a fair share in the American dream.

Since the repeal of the Chinese Exclusion Act in 1943, Chinese have made great strides in reclaiming what was previously kept away from them—an opportunity to partake in the wealth of possibilities offered by America, and to claim their own success stories alongside other groups. This process has been particularly accelerated by the immigrant selection process initiated by the Immigration Act of 1965, which allowed a huge number of highly educated, elite members of Chinese society to enter the United States during the second half of the twentieth century. Trained to serve as leaders and to drive industrial development and technological innovation in a modern society, these top-of-the-line professionals could easily find a niche in the American economy, which made their upward mobility on the average much faster than that of the largely working-class immigrant groups of European stock. Statistically, then, many Chinese have achieved in one generation what others couldn't in several.

But, at the other end of the social scale, new unskilled Chinese immigrants continue to pour into the United States in unprecedented numbers, thanks to the family union provisions of the 1965 immigration law. Their experience is vastly different from that of their privileged fellow Chinese, and their social mobility will follow the more typical immigrant pattern: they will work extremely hard and sacrifice without adequate reward, in order to provide better opportunities for their children.

The earlier generation of artists who immigrated to the United States from China experimented with the East-meets-West paradigm in rather timid, restrained ways, and more often than not remained bound by tradition. Artists like Chen Chi found anchor and inspiration in China's great classics (see poem in the front of this book). Xu Bing belongs to a new generation of iconoclasts, whose strength lies precisely in their ability to mock and debunk that age-old tradition. His installation, *A Book From Heaven,* consists of an entire room covered with reels of a giant-sized Chinese classic. The huge sheets of book-print on rice paper look like the genuine article until a closer examination reveals that the artist has made up his own vocabulary of mock Chinese characters, which are quite meaningless, and carved them into wood blocks to create a mock classic—a true classic for the new millennium.

The growing Chinese presence in many communities throughout the United States has created a new awareness of their potential to influence electoral politics through voting blocs and strategies—something the younger generation is already beginning to exploit to its advantage. The ability of affluent Chinese Americans to influence electoral politics through fund-raising and donations to parties and candidates has also not gone unnoticed.

All too often, the way Chinese Americans are perceived and treated in the United States continues to be shaped by the way Americans see China. And that continues to depend on how the United States government defines its national interests vis-à-vis the "sleeping giant" of the Asian continent, which has by turns been a resource, a market, an ally, a friend, and the deadliest of enemies.

But ongoing discrimination should not cloud the achievements of the Chinese who have made the United States their home, as our text and pictures show. Like all immigrant groups who have come to America's "Gold Mountain"—whether propelled quickly up its socio-economic slopes or hobbled by the prejudice of the majority—the Chinese Americans have been profoundly affected by their adopted country. And though marginalized and mistreated, they have managed, through toil, ingenuity, and determination, to leave an indelible mark on America and what it means to be American.

For the last two decades, the restructuring of China's economy has sent an ever-increasing number of illegal immigrants to the United States, in search of golden opportunities not available at home. Due to their tenuous status and enormous debts, these newcomers are driven to work at practically any cost. Their bitter predicament, often compared to indentured servitude, conjures images of turn-of-the-century Chinatowns, and negates the progress made by their countrymen since the civil rights movement. Their presence accentuates divisions within the Chinese-American community.

Yet it is precisely these divisions that promise to make the Chinese-American experience a typical American one, in which employment, education, and social security concerns override ethnic and race allegiances, and success is measured in individual terms. New generations of Chinese immigrants are already creating success stories of their own. In the short span of just a few decades, their academic and professional successes have elevated them to the status of a "model minority"—a construct which, however flawed, nevertheless recognizes their undeniable achievements. More importantly, this collective success has given many individuals the license to dream and venture into areas most Chinese would have never entered just a short while ago. And, if there is any certainty in numbers, with the Chinese population in the United States doubling every ten years, more and bigger dreams are yet to come.

(Above) At the close of the twentieth century America finds itself in the midst of a renewed interest in things Chinese. The new economic prosperity in China and other East Asian nations with significant Chinese populations has once again brought the two continents together; this time in a new paradigm called "The Pacific Rim." It is an imagined realm that spans the Pacific Ocean, where economic and political interests intersect, people intermingle, and cultures cross-pollinate to the benefit of all. On the American side, this has resulted in an unprecedented influx of investment and people, and an adjustment in the public life of many coastal cities. Vancouver in British Columbia, Canada, has been in the forefront of this booming exchange. To accommodate its rapidly increasing Chinese community, the city constructed the first Chinese full-scale classical scholar's garden outside China in 1986, and named it Dr. Sun Yat-sen Classical Chinese Garden. The so-called "scholar's gardens" flourished in the urban centers of southern China during the Sung and Ming dynasties as venues where wealthy merchants and scholar-officials could escape the bustling world of commerce and politics to find harmony with nature. The gardens use water, rocks, plants, and architectural structures to create idealized landscapes contained within cloistering white walls, where a city-dweller can find a moment of peace and tranquillity to engage in quiet contemplation. Some 90,000 visitors stop by the one in Vancouver every year.

(Above) The cities of Portland, Oregon; Seattle, Washington; and San Francisco, California, are planning to open their own classical Chinese scholar's gardens in the near future. On the East Coast, one was opened on Staten Island in New York City in August 1999. Photo © Corky Lee.

CHINESE SITES ON THE INTERNET

GENEALOGY:

1. Chinese Immigration and Chinese in the United States: Records in the Regional Archives of the National Archives and Records Administration

http://www.nara.gov/regional/findaids/chirip.html

Records of immigrants from the exclusion period often show only adopted names. On this page, you can search cemetery records to find the true surnames of your ancestors. Also includes a brief history of the exclusion period.

2. Columbia University's C.V. Starr East Asian Library

http://http://www.cc.columbia.edu/cu/libraries/indiv/east-asian/

Includes a list of electronic resources on Chinese regions and culture. Also allows limited access to family histories from the Ming and Qing dynasties.

3. The USGenWeb Project-Home Page

http://www.usgenweb.com

US Genealogy Project—Track down records of your Chinese-American ancestors.

4. Genealogy-Home Page (about.com)

http://genealogy.about.com

About.com's Genealogy site.

5. RootsWeb Genealogical Data Cooperative

http://www.rootsweb.com

Genealogical mailing lists, home pages, and search engines. Subscriptions range from free to $24 per year depending on level of service.

6. GenTree

http://www.gentree.com

Links to all known genealogical databases searchable through the Web.

7. Helm's Genealogy Toolbox-Providing the Tools to Research Your Family History Online

http://www.genealogytoolbox.com

Resources include: links to genealogical resources, news articles, guide to genealogical software, pages for posting research questions, a genealogical bookstore, and a site to register your own genealogical homepage.

SCHOLARLY & HISTORICAL INFORMATION:

8. Asian American Studies Library at the University of California, Berkeley

http://eslibrary.berkeley.edu/aaslhome.html

An excellent resource for scholars and students of the Asian American experience.

9. Asian History, Chinese History, Chinese Americans, Asians, San Francisco History, California History

http://www.a-better.com/LK-AHSTY.HTM

Includes pictorial histories of many aspects of the Chinese immigrant experience. Scores more points for content than for design.

10. Model Minority

http://www.itp.berkeley.edu/~asam121/model_minority/model_minority.html

Arguments against the "model minority myth."

11. Traditional Chinese Medicine in Chinese-American Communities

http://www.camsociety.org/issues/Attitudes.htm

An extensive/exhaustive article on this subject.

12. China: Dim Sum: A Connection to Chinese-American Culture

http://www.newton.mec.edu/Angier/DimSum/china dimsumaconnection.html

A cross curricula, integrated resource for elementary classrooms which enhances awareness and understanding of Chinese-American culture while building basic academic skills.

13. Chinese New Year

http://deil.lang.uiuc.edu/web.pages/holidays/ ChineseNewYear.html

Everything you ever wanted to know about this holiday.

14. American Anti-Chinese History Timeline

http://www.sinocast.com/sinocast/anti_chinese.html

A timeline of injustices perpetrated against Chinese Americans. (Note: The site on which this is hosted, *http://www.sinocast.com*, is also an interesting resource—"Chinese Web TV News.")

15. AskAsia.org

http://www.askasia.org/who_we_are/wwa_frame.htm

An exciting, informative on-line source K-12 Asian and Asian American studies. Offers access to high-quality, classroom-tested resources and cultural information, engaging games and activities, and links to relevant people, places, and institutions.

16. Chinese American Identity

http://www.owlnet.rice.edu/~jenlin/HIST310/main.html

A well-made report on the Chinese-American immigrant experience by a group of students at Rice University. However, there's no guarantee these pages will continue to exist once the students graduate . . .

ONLINE GALLERIES & EXHIBITS:

17. China the Beautiful

http://www.chinapage.org

This page is designed to be "like visiting the Chinese gallery in an art museum."

18. The Chinese Historical Society of America

http://www.chsa.org

Includes some exhibits of fine art, among other things.

19. CHCP Virtual Museum & Library

http://www.chcp.org/Pvirtual.html

The Chinese Historical and Cultural Project.

20. The Promise of Gold Mountain: Tucson's Chinese Heritage

http://www.library.arizona.edu/images/chamer/chinese.html

An excellent online historical exhibit.

ORGANIZATIONS:

21. Organizaion of Chinese Americans (OCA)

http://www.ocanatl.org

22. Committee of 100: Homepage

http://www.committee100.org

Members address important issues concerning the Chinese-American community, as well as issues affecting U.S.-China relations.

23. Asian American Arts Foundation

http://www.aaafoundation.com

This group states its purpose to be: "to create greater awareness and consciousness of the need to support the arts and provide ongoing financial support to help support the work of Asian Pacific artists and arts organizations."

24. Taiwanese American Foundation (TAF) Info Page

http://member.aol.com/TAFInfo/

25. Chinese American Political Association

http://www.capa-news.org

The Chinese American Political Association (CAPA) is a non-partisan, non-profit, educational, and political organization of the Chinese-American community in the San Francisco Bay Area.

REGIONAL:

26. San Diego's Chinese Community

http://www.sandiegoonline.com/forums/chinese/chinese1.htm

Much of the information on this site is region-specific, as the title indicates. However, there is some content that would be interesting to Chinese Americans anywhere. Includes the San Diego Chinese Historical Museum, free recipies, a "Dear Confucius Q&A," and many other links.

27. Chinese Culture Center of San Francisco

http://www.c-c-c.org

A major community-based, nonprofit organization established in 1965 to foster the understanding and appreciation of Chinese and Chinese-American art, history, and culture in the United States.

MISCELLANEOUS:

28. GoldSea -- The Asian American Supersite

http://www.goldsea.com

The authors' personal favorite Asian-American web site.

29. Jade Magazine Online

http://www.jademagazine.com

A magazine for young Asian women.

30. ABCs for ABCs

http://www.geocities.com/Athens/Parthenon/9282/

The latter set of "ABC"s stands for "American-Born Chinese." Not a children's site, despite the title.

31. About.com's Chinese Culture Home Page

http://chineseculture.about.com

For Chinese-American web surfers to learn more about the culture of their heritage.

32. About.com's Asian-American Culture Home Page

http://asianamculture.about.com

About.com also has a site related directly to the Asian American experience. The content appears to be updated pretty frequently, so repeat visits would not go unrewarded.

33. Taiwan WWW VL

http://peacock.tnjc.edu.tw/taiwan-wwwvl.html

The Taiwan Virtual Library is filled with Chinese-related, and in particular Taiwan-related information. It's in English, despite the fact that it's being served out of China.

34. Asian Studies WWW Virtual Library

http://coombs.anu.edu.au/WWWVL-AsianStudies.html

35. Chinese Culture Online Library

http://www.brainlink.com/~kkin/ccolold.html

A New York based nonprofit virtual library, dedicated to Chinese culture.

36. H-GIG Asian American History

http://www.ucr.edu/h-gig/hist-topics/asian.html

A collection of links to Asian American history-related pages/sites.

37. ABC Maps of China; Flag, Map, Economy, Geography, Climate, Natural Resources, Current Issues, International Agreements, Population, Social Statistics, Political System

http://www.theodora.com/maps/china_map.html

Maps of China.

38. Immigration USA

http://www.immigration-usa.com

Immigration USA is a software package designed to help with U.S. immigration law. The site is designed primarily to market the software, but it does include information, and a discussion forum, related to the subject of immigration.

39. Shen's Books and Supplies-Online Catalog-Chinese American

http://www.shens.com/subjects/Chinese+American.htm

Extensive reading list, all about Chinese Americans. Broken down by sub-category, with brief descriptions of each book, and links to buy.

40. Encyclopedia Mythica: Chinese mythology

http://www.pantheon.org/mythica/areas/chinese/

An encyclopedia of terms from Chinese mythology.

41. A S I A C E N T R A L

http://www.asiacentral.com

"Your Asian American Connection"

42. ABCFLASH

http://www.abcflash.com

"The Premier Website for Asian American News and Entertainment."

43. Asia Society

http://www.asiasociety.org

"America's leading institution dedicated to fostering understanding of Asia and communication between Americans and the people of Asia and the Pacific." Lots of content in different areas.

44. amagazine.com-Inside Asian America

http://www.amagazine.com

45. yolk.com

http://www.yolk.com

The electronic magazine about Asian American pop culture, experience, and influence.

ONLINE COMMUNITIES:

46. AsianAvenue.com

http://www.asianavenue.com

The Internet's first interactive community for Asian Americans.

47. AsiangURLs.com—website for women of Asian heritage

http://www.asiangurls.com

Strives to be a web-community for women of Asian cultures and promote the interests of Asian and Asian American women. Emphasizes, in the light of its web address, that it is not a pornographic site.

48. CCCChat Home Page (English)

http://www.cccchat.com

Supports both English and Big 5 Chinese. Features resident-created chat room, E.T. Talk, U & I live chat. (That's a total of 4 "c"s in "cccchat." Type it incorrectly and we will not be held responsible for where you wind up.)

49. the Asian Community Online Network @igc

http://www.igc.apc.org/acon

50. Asian American e-mailing lists

http://www.liszt.com/lists.cgi?word=asian+american&junk=s&an=all

This page will direct you to e-mail listservs on various subjects of interest to Asian Americans.

51. ChinaWorldLink-Chinese and Taiwanese chat, personals, games, news, Hong Kong, travel, music, culture

http://www.chinaworldlink.com

Another online community for Chinese worldwide.

CHINESE-LANGUAGE SITES:

52. Chinese Cyber City—Largest Chinese Community

http://www1.ccchome.com/index.htm

An online community for Chinese around the world. The site is written mostly in Chinese, so web surfers who speak English only are, alas, out of luck.

53. SINA.com US—#1 Destination Site for Chinese Worldwide

http://home.sina.com/index.html

Another site entirely in Chinese. Looks big and important.

54. CANEWS

http://www.asialinksinc.com/newspaper/index.html

CA News calls itself the "Voice of Chinese Americans." The majority of the site appears to be in Chinese language, so the news on this site will only be available to those who can read Chinese.

55. Hugh Lauter Levin Associates Chinese Links

http://www.HLLA.com/reference/chineselinks.html

The list of links from this very book is on the publisher's web site (at *http://www.HLLA.com*), so that if you don't want to type in all these links (or carry the book around with you), you can go to our page and click on any of them.

INDEX

PHOTO CREDITS

Courtesy *A. Magazine*: p. 226

Courtesy American Antiquarian Society: pp. 40, 42–43, 47

Balch Institute Library: Building the Gold Mountain, Philadelphia, Chinatown: p. 183; Holy Redeemer Chinese Catholic Church Photographs: pp. 146 (above), 158, 161; Mary E. Scott Chinese Sunday School, First Baptist Church Photographs: p. 150

Archive Photos: pp. 49, 54, 56, 58, 69, 79, 80–81, 91, 136, 137 (both), 138 (left), 140 (above), 141, 148, 159, 160, 205 (above), 208–209; American Stock: pp. 44, 50, 59, 60, 135; Blank Archives: p. 78; Camera Press Ltd: p. 163; Fotos International: p. 194; Jeff Greenberg: pp. 180–181; © 1991 H. David Hartman: pp. 184–185 (background); © A. Kachaturian/ Saga: p. 216–217; MGM: p. 140 (left); Sonia Moskowitz/Archive Newsphotos: p. 204; Popperfoto: p. 134; Reuters: p. 205 (right); Reuters/John Gibbins: p. 191; Reuters/Jay Gorodetzer: p. 227 (right); Reuters/Brian Snyder: p. 215; Reuters/Andrew Wong: p. 227 (left); © Joan Slatkin: p. 198–199; 20th Century-Fox: p. 138 (above); United Artists: p. 223; Santi Visalli Inc.: pp. 130–131, 184 (inset)

California Department of Parks and Recreation: p. 128

Courtesy of the California History Room, California State Library, Sacramento, CA: pp. 55, 72, 73

Lia Chang Gallery: © 1994: pp. 200, 224, back cover; © 1995: pp. 203, 206 (right), 219; © 1996: pp. 195, 202, 220 (left); © 1997: p. 206 (left); © 1999: p. 207 (right)

Collection The Connecticut Historical Society: p. 48

Corbis-Bettmann: pp. 28, 33, 38–39, 41, 67, 77, 103, 108, 178; Arnold Genthe: p. 103; Kevin R. Morris: pp. 14–15; Baldwin H. Ward: p. 35; UPI: pp. 132, 145, 151, 153, 155, 214

© Deborah Feingold/Corbis Outline, 7/98: p. 177

Idaho State Historical Society: pp. 57, 71, 106–107, 118, 119

Courtesy Cai jin: p. 228

© Corky Lee: pp. 164, 165, 166, 167, 168, 171, 172–173, 188, 189, 197, 207 (below), 225, 231 (bottom)

Library of Congress: pp. 26 (both), 27, 51, 52, 61, 62, 65, 75, 82, 84, 85, 86, 87, 90, 92, 93, 97, 101, 104, 110–111, 115, 117, 123, 129, 142, 146 (left), 149; AP Photo, NYWTS Collection: p. 147; Bain Collection: p. 127; Arnold Genthe Collection: Front cover, 88, 98, 109, 112 (both), 113; Original photo by Carleton Watkins: p. 68

Magnum Photos Inc.: Chien-Chi Chang, © 1996: pp. 10, 13, 182, 186–187, © 1998: pp. 12, 174; Alex Webb, © 1989: p. 179; Patrick Zachman, © 1987: p. 176

The Metropolitan Museum of Art, © 1980: p. 23

Museum of Chinese in the Americas: pp. 102, 105, 192 (both)

National Archives: pp. 95, 125, 129, 143, 156

New York Public Library Picture Collection: pp. 34, 36–37

Peabody Essex Museum, Salem, MA: Mark Sexton: pp. 16, 21, 24–25, 30–31

Robert Reichert: p. 212

Lynn Rosenthal: p. 193 [*Eagle,* by Chen Xue Ken, made of magazines, toilet paper, wire, glue, paint. Private collection]

The Society for the Preservation of New England Antiquities: p. 53

Courtesy of South Dakota Historical Society— State Archives, John C.H. Grabill: p. 63

Stanford University News Service, L.A. Cicero: p. 213

Tombstone, Arizona: pp. 120, 121

The UT Institute of Texan Cultures at San Antonio: p. 122

Courtesy Vera Wang: pp. 221

Timothy White/Sony: p. 210

Courtesy Yahoo!: p. 218

Courtesy Dr. Sun Yat-sen Garden, Vancouver, B.C.: p. 231 (top)

Courtesy Martin Yan: p. 220 (right)

Wyoming Division of Cultural Resources: p. 100